Hessett: Portrait of a Suffolk village

By
Brenda Picking

Acknowledgements

Thanks must go to the people who have given up their time to talk and provide information about themselves and the village.

Thank you to the late Ron Gant, Ken Hoxley and Frank Whitnall, Elizabeth Nicholson and all the staff at the Bury St Edmunds branch of the Suffolk Record Office, especially Liz Wigmore and Clive Paine and also Jill Carter without whose guidance this book would not have been possible.
Thank you also to my long suffering husband for his patience and help.

Dedication

In memory of Don Picking
1932 - 2018
who provided the encouragement
and support to produce this book

Published 2020

ISBN: 978-1-8381461-5-3

Printed by Gipping Press Ltd, Needham Market, Suffolk

Contents

Introduction

RESEARCHING the village has been a fascinating and frustrating journey. After many hours of research and walking around the village and preparing a profile it is very difficult to make sure that everything that can be found is included, but I hope that what has been included will be of interest to the reader.

This history of the village does not profess to be exhaustive. In the 14th Century everything that was needed by villagers was kept or made within the village. In the following centuries a trip to the nearest town made for a day out whether to trade or buy items. Life is dramatically different in the modern day.

There are many books and documents that have been written about the church, but very little on the actual village. There is a short chapter on the church with a list of the Rectors and their patrons. We then come to a chapter about World War 1 and how the men suffered under difficult conditions.

Then we have the village from the Doomsday Survey of 1086 to as near to the present day as possible. There is a chapter on the families who were the first families recorded as living in Hessett. This has been taken from the website Rootsweb.com and also from the Wills kept in the Bury Record Office. After which we come to the village population and to those who were farming and in other occupations, with the farmhouses and oldest houses recorded.

Next is a sad time reflected with the Workhouse and the ailments the inhabitants lived with, we then come to the prison or correction house, for some of the men sent to prison or transported, they were just trying to feed the family. The local inn and telephone exchange are next with the earliest phone numbers being obtained by the shops and the gentry of the village. Then there is recreation and there was a lot happening in the early 1900's. The last chapter is the memories of village people, some of whom are no longer with us. Also added are some extra photos of the village, and maps the earliest found is 1783 to after 1904.

Brenda Picking

Hessett: 'The settlers within the hedges'

THE FIRST mention of the parish of Hessett is in the reign of King Ethelred II, A.D. 1005. Ulfketel, who was Earl of East Anglia, gave the villages of Hessett, Rougham and Bradfield to the Abbey of St Edmund.

Hedgesette is one of nine villages found in Norfolk and Suffolk having the suffix "Setan" or "Sett" meaning "settlers". Hegesete, an earlier spelling, may have been the home of an early "Hice" or "Higg" family, old English names the forerunners of today's "Hicks" and "Hickson". A large tract of land in the parish is called Hicket or Hicket's Heath. Hege signifies an enclosed ground and if a villager chose to settle upon enclosed ground away from the 'tun' or village he and his people might be called Hegesetan, "Settlers at Hege". There was one manor in Hessett and this belonged to Bury Abbey in the middle ages (being a subdivision of their manor of Rougham). The moated site at the back of Mount Close is known as "Old Hall" and according to the Suffolk Archaeology Site and Monuments records was larger than Hessett Hall in 1723.

In Anglo-Saxon times those who made their homes north of the River Waveney called themselves North Folk, while those who remained between the River Waveney and the River Stour became known as the South Folk, hence Norfolk and Suffolk were born.

At the time of the Domesday Survey of 1086 AD, Hessett was owned jointly by the Abbey and Frodo, Abbot Baldwin's brother, and seems for all civil purposes to have been a part of the Manor of Rougham with a population of 76. Although the Abbot of Bury was the 'lord' of Hessett he had several wealthy tenants, among whom in the 1280s was William de Stanham, John de Herst, Roger son of Geoffrey, Walter de Wlfhal and John de Beumond.

In general when you read about villages they are very much the same so when reading this about Hessett it could be any village in the county. Hessett was partly arable and partly pasture as there were shepherds, cow men and game-keepers, so one can assume that there was livestock kept by some farmers. One mile to the north is Beyton which is now accessible to the A14. The boundary of Hessett was noted by the first big oak tree in the grounds of Beyton House between the two villages. The road at Hicket Heath to Freecroft Farm was the west boundary, reported to be part of a Roman road. The Blackbourn Brook marks the south boundary and farm land lies to the east. The land is heavy and is loam and clay with a clay subsoil. The chief crops were wheat, oats, barley and beans.

Agricultural labourers were the backbone of English life, but for them life was very hard. Under the open field system, the arable land was usually in three large fields, each field divided into strips. Every year the villagers decided what to plant in each field and usually left one field fallow. The common was used by villagers to graze animals.

The Hoo family settled in Hessett in 1286 AD, Sir Robert Hoo is believed to be the first (ref: Materials for a History of Hessett by William Cooke, 1877). Twenty-five years later the Abbot of Bury St Edmunds is styled "the Capital Lord of Hessett".

In 1327 William Fynch, William de Stonham, George son of Thomas, Nicholas dil Brok and John Bacon appear as tax-payers. At the Dissolution of the abbey in 1539, when pensions were assigned to the discharged monks, two were Hessett men, Robtus Hegsett, alias Potkyn and Thomas Hegsett alias Rowght. The Parish Registers started in 1539, the year following the issue of Thomas Cromwell's injunction concerning them. During the earlier years the entries of the families of Hoo and Bacon are very numerous, and later came the Le Heup family.

The Advowson (the right to appoint Rectors) was held with the Manor by the Abbey until the Dissolution, the Monasteries were granted with the Manor in 1541 to Thomas Bacon of Hessett by Henry VIII. It remained in the possession of that family until 1653.

Widespread riots occurred in the early 19th century as the price of bread rose. Soldiers returning from the Napoleonic Wars were looking for work. Bread would have been the main stay of the working person's meal, but with food prices rising, widespread hardship was felt.

During the late 18th and early 19th centuries Enclosure Acts were widespread and much common land was enclosed and this caused hardship for poorer people. For the small farmer and the cottager it could mean ruin as they lost their common rights. All over the country, poorer people were forced to become labourers, and deprived of sources of their pre-enclosure income, they now had to survive on a wage earned by working for the bigger farmer. They supplemented their wages with fuel such as wood from waste lands, and possibly a cow or pig in the garden and what crops they could grow themselves.

In the 1830s machinery such as threshing machines were introduced, depriving workers of jobs, and more riots occurred and the machines were destroyed or put out of action. These became known as the 'Swing Riots', as the thresher would swing backwards and forwards to separate the corn from the husk.

Around the same time as the agricultural labourers' incomes were shrinking, the price of food was growing. The cost of poultry, pork, milk and cheese rose immediately after Enclosure. Meat and cheese, once part of the labourer's diet, were now luxuries. Prevented from leaving because of the Settlement laws under the Old Poor Law, this made moving difficult as everyone had only one parish where they had settlement and were therefore entitled to parish relief. As a result of this there were food riots all over the country; there was hardly a county where there was not disorder.

In the 1840s wages were about 8s (40p) or 9s (45p) a week, or less in some cases, and some villagers might have lived in tied cottages which would mean if they lost their job, they would also lose their home.

The machinery used was all worked by hand. The plough would have been pulled by a horse or ox, and the worker walked behind (if only they had had a pedometer), so it took a long time to get a field ready for the crops to be planted. When harvesting the crop it would have been cut by scythe, tied and placed into sheaves then put together, corn head upwards, until ready to be made into a haystack.

A lot of farmers employed children and pay for them was low, but it helped the family. The children were employed to scare the birds from the fields when the harvesting was over, also when seeds were sown in winter and spring. If an employee had helped to bring in the harvest then the wife and children would have the right to glean the field, after every ear of corn had been collected. Another job for the children was stone picking, collecting stones when the harvest was over and before ploughing and sowing of the next crop began. It was a disliked job and paid by the bushel of stones collected, which were then used to make road surfaces.

A worker's day started at first light and finished when it was dark, so summer would have been long days while winter would have been shorter. The work during the winter would have been doing odd jobs that there was not time for during the harvest.

In 1840 with wages low and unemployment high, many houses were in poor condition and living was very hard. How the family survived would have been down to the father growing some vegetables in a small garden, and possibly poaching rabbits and small game.

Between 1842 and 1851 there were quite a lot of arson attacks, the burning of haystacks, barns filled with grain and even machinery. In 1844 there were 47 attacks in Suffolk, and in 1845 there were 16 in the county. The people probably thought that they were getting back at the "rich farmers", but in reality they were hurting themselves and their fellow workers, as with no hay or corn there would be no hay to feed the cattle or to sell and no corn to sell or use for the next crops.

In 1874 the labourers went on strike when they asked for a pay rise and the farmers refused. The strike spread all over the country, but after a while families who had no money coming in were forced to go back to work. However, the Agricultural Union, formed in 1872, provided a voice for the workers.

When the Education Act of 1876 came in all children up to the age of 14 had to go to school, but with a lot of the families being poor the children were either not sent to school or the school closed early so that children could earn a little money to help their parents.

At the turn of the 20th century, according to information in Kelly's Directories, Hessett was an attractive village of thatched and red tinted cottages, one of which bears the date 1743, where little bridges cross the ditches to the front doors. The village is 2.5 miles from Thurston, 5.5 miles east of Bury St Edmunds and 93 miles from London. In 1881 there were 428 inhabitants and comprised 1568 acres of land.

Hessett was in the Thedwastre (also known as Thedwestry) Hundred, now Mid Suffolk, and the polling district was Woolpit. Petty session divisions for Hessett were under Thingoe and Thedwastre and met every Wednesday, 12 noon at Shire Hall, Bury St Edmunds. In 1848 the local school was built at the north end of the village. There were two greens; one was Rans Green, called Wrens Green on the 1743 map (Ref E3/30/13.1), with the main village green being in the centre, now only the main green exists.

Rural life between 1800 and 1960 was a period of changes in the way that village people lived and worked, while at the same time maintaining a strong sense of community and tradition. Most villages had water pumps and many homes had their own wells, or shared one with their neighbours, but most water used in the home had to be carried inside in buckets.

At the turn of the 20th century many villages were centred on a large country estate that provided work and accommodation for local men and women. Villages thrived, as many people were able to secure employment in the vicinity. It was a time when grand houses still employed legions of staff, and in tiny village communities the benevolence of the local gentry might affect a large proportion of its inhabitants.

Then there were the farms. Farming was still largely un-mechanised and a vast workforce was required for tasks that, within a few short years, would be done by machine alone. At harvesting or haymaking, people would come from all around the village to lend a hand, whether they worked on the farm or not, their ages ranged from children to grandparents. It was almost as though rural people had an inherent instinct, handed down through the generations, to help the farmer make hay or harvest his corn before the winter weather set in. Also in the long school holidays, older boys couldn't wait to get to work to earn some money. Many villages also had a mill, bakery, slaughterhouse or smithy, all of which provided work.

World War I brought changes to village life. Following the war, during the 1920s and 1930s, younger men had to make up the workforce for the soldiers that had been so cruelly taken away. In the 1920s, too, changes began to occur that would have a profound effect on village life. The decline of stately homes and the country houses, accompanied by rapidly improving farming technology, meant that fewer jobs were available.

However, not everything was mechanised. The decline of jobs in the village itself coincided with transport improvements, enabling villagers to make train or bus journeys into local towns for work, and later, motorcycles and cars further aided the independence of villagers.

In the 1930s the countryside was still widely farmed by small independent farmers and many of them ran their own local dairies delivering milk from a horse and cart. Horace Ottley from Hessett delivered the milk from Grange Farm, Beyton. He rode a trike with a cart on the front, but was killed early in 1938 near the White Horse, Beyton. Mr Sharman then took over delivering the milk by trike until he bought a van.

Nearly every village had its own shop, some villages had several selling everything imaginable. If life in general was slightly less hectic in bygone days, shopping was an even more relaxing experience. There was no point being in a hurry to get served. The shopkeeper took his time, weighing, measuring, cutting and individually bagging up all the purchased goods. The shop was also a place for gossip and a chat.

In 1929, the world entered the Great Depression. It was a terrible time for everyone but particularly for those in villages. By the mid-1930s things had slowly recovered, just in time for the next major event; World War II. In the countryside farming became intensive, and tranquil villages were transformed into bustling communities. Hordes of Land Army Girls worked in the fields, the Home Guard was started and shared between Beyton and Hessett, meeting at the White Horse, Beyton. Then there was the evacuation scheme, when children from towns and cities were relocated to the countryside.

Articles from the Bury Free Press reveal how people were supporting the war effort. In January 1939: whist drives in aid of the Hospital special appeal fund in the Church room and from Marlow & Co an Air Raid Shelter, No 1, could be bought for only £7 10s - £7.50 today. Another article from February 1940: the first sixpenny whist drive was held in the Church Room in aid of the comforts for the troops fund with 10½ tables being occupied, but no mention of how much was made. On 4th March 1940 an article said a series of whist drives were to be held in the Church Room. On October 30th 1942 is an article about the Hessett collection for the Red Cross Penny-a-Week Fund which realised £2.0s.3d. The collectors were Misses Deane Bullett, Joyce Willis, Doreen Davey and Beryl Frost. Also is a report on the knitting club, knitting socks, scarves, balaclavas and gloves for the troops.

From the parish records (Ref EF500/1/7) and in 1933 each electric pylon cost £19, in 1946 an electric cable was put between Rougham and Hessett. The £72 cost was shared between Spring Farm, Shrubbery Farm and Lane Farm. It cost an extra £25 to have the wires connected into the house.

From the Bury Post March 28th 1946, was a report of a Mr W E Blizzard, Civil Engineer, who attended a meeting and gave a report on the progress made with trial borings for water. He expressed the opinion that the council would have to provide bored wells for the houses until a piped water supply became available. He undertook to look into the question of providing sewage disposal schemes for Hessett. It is believed piped water came to the village around 1947 although no specific date can be found. Mains drainage was bought into the village in 1966.

Buildings old and new

The Street
Although a lot of new homes have been built in the village there are many old houses that are Grade II listed and the church is a Grade I listed building. For properties named Grade II listed the information is recorded in "The Society for the Protection of Ancient Buildings", dated 15th November 1954, and can be found in the Bury St Edmunds Record Office.

The first two Local Housing Association houses built in The Street were completed in 1935 (Ref EF500/1/30). The Street was originally called Church Street in 1696. Other Local Housing Association houses in Hessett were completed in Beyton Road in 1950, with the bungalows being completed in 1953 (Ref EF500/1/34).

The houses in Beyton Road were built in the early 1950s.

Taking a look at the houses not already down on paper there is Fordacre which was originally two cottages and where Mr Bidwell lived in one side of the cottages; he cut wood from Shavers Wood in Beyton and sold faggots and hurdles.

Next to Five Bells Cottage where Lime Tree close is now, were allotments with a ditch in front and a pond near where Pipers Cottage stands now. There were also allotments at the end of Beyton Road and up on the Heath for use of the villagers who did not have very big gardens or needed more space to grow more food for the family. The only allotments left now are up at the Heath.

East View was a pork butchers and Post Office, which then moved to The Old Post Office nearby. Where Laurel Dene is now was a sweet shop run by Mabel and Alex Renson. Opposite the shop was the Mission Hall, and Mr Ruben Renson was the Roadman. The Cottage named Wilwyn had sheds in the garden and the gentleman who lived there bred mink.

The Green

The Local Housing Association houses on The Green near the telephone box were completed in 1932 (Ref EF500/1/30). Where Brindle House stands were two sheds; there was one at the front of the land, and in the shed at the back was where Mr Halls made coffins as he was the undertaker who lived in The Guildhall, now Guildhall Cottage. Later on Mr Dick Renson had a lorry which was parked in the front shed as the undertakers had long since disappeared.

Further up the road at No. 4 The Bungalow, on the 1892 map to the 1904 map was where the forge was situated. Mr Hubbard dealt with horses that needed shoeing and mended the carts and carriages. The forge was pulled down for a house built and later made way for the Bungalows. 1 and 2 The Bungalows were completed in 1953 and 3 and 4 were finished in 1956 (Ref EF500/1/34).

Vine Cottage, right, was where the cobbler Mr Bland lived who had his workshop to the left hand side of the house as you face the house. Where Beech Paddocks are now there were two cottages which were pulled down after 1904. Mrs Gertie Sturgeon lived in one side; and in the other were Mr and Mrs Chettleburgh with their son James,  Nellie Blake and Harold Clark. The family of Mrs Sturgeon were moved into the new local association houses built opposite in 1935. Further up the Green near to Spring Farm some more houses were built and completed in 1949.

Up Hubbards Lane in the 1800s, to the right of Valentines Way, the track was known as Honeypot Lane as this was where a gentleman with a pony and trap would empty the latrines of the village. Up the lane was a building called Old House and The Park was down the left track and this side of Drinkstone Lake. Some of the houses in Valentines Way are where Mr Valentine had his house and sheds, now long since gone. There was also a gravel pit taking out gravel for runways and roads, the rest of the houses are where Lane Farm used to be. Mr and Mrs Godden lived in one cottage and Mr Godden was the scout leader. The scouts met in a tin outhouse on the side of the house before a room was added onto the Village Hall.

Heath Road

There was a pond at the side of the green in Heath Road with a railing round it where, I have been told, children used to play. Although some of the village floods nowadays the photo below shows Heath Road flooded in 1970.

Going up Heath Road on the right is The Laurels. There stood two cottages which were burnt down by a firework which caught the thatch alight. They then put two caravans in their place and Mrs Nellie Blake lived in one looking after Mr Baldry who lived in the other. The caravans were then replaced by a wooden bungalow, and when Mrs Blake passed away the bungalow was pulled down and a house erected on the site.

After the house was built an extra room was added which became the butchers, when that closed the butchers moved to where Chapel Cottage is, next to Alwyd. Woodcroft was the field of the Sawyer where he kept his wood and Heath Close was The Timber Yard Field.

Hurdle Cottage, built in 1723 from the deeds, was where the hurdle maker lived. There were originally three cottages; Hurdle Cottage and the middle cottage were made into one. The other cottage May Cottage, was a laundry. There is a letter from 1867 from the Rector, Henry Bunbury Blake, showing the houses were exempt from any Tithe Rent charge, and another letter from 1927 showing the market value to be £140.

Completed in 1939 were Association Houses in Heath Road. They were lived in by T Cocksedge, P Piper, F Bloomfield and W Catchpole (Ref EF500/1/31). Some of the Association houses were renovated, three in all and four were demolished and rebuilt at The Green in 1939 (Ref EF500/1/35).

In 1977 to celebrate the Queen's Silver Jubilee the village held a fete and a fancy dress parade for the children. They were judged and then taken around the village on the trailer at the back of Martin Bauly's tractor sitting on hay bales; the weather was cold and wet.

During the 1960s and 1980s there was a Ladies Club held in the old Village Hall. Most of the ladies of the village joined and met for talks and outings. It was started by the Rector's wife, Maureen Marsh, and was originally held in the Rectory.

The first record of the Parish Council is in 1894. We have a photo of the Hessett Parish Council in 1908, most of the people are known. In 1908 the Parish Council met in the School Room. Those attending were Mr Squirrell, Rev. Jones, Mrs Bauly, Mr Raker, Mr Ottley, Mr Woodward and Mr Green. Mr Moore was the clerk. The Parish Council later met in the Church Room but when repairs started on 29th March 1921, the meetings moved back to the School Room for several years until the work was completed in 1926.

There is also a photo of the Parish Council taken in 2010; they are (back row) Theresa Worley, Debbie Stringer, Janice Gibson, Brian Jones and Chris Glass; front row Graham Bauly, Eileen Seaman (clerk) and Maggie Durrant.

Members of Hessett Parish Council in 2010.

More recently ….

There was a Millennium Committee set up around the year 2000 which organised events including an annual Bonfire Night firework display.

The Village Hall, which was renovated in 2016, hosts a coffee morning every third Thursday of the month, the Friendly Club – a lunch club – on the second and fourth Tuesdays in the month and on Monday mornings there are Pilates classes to help people with their flexibility and movement.

The Hessett Church Preservation Society (formerly The Friends of Hessett Church) is raising money for badly needed repairs in the church through its membership subscriptions and events.

In 2007 and 2008 Carenza Lewis and associates from Cambridge University Department of Archaeology came to the village to dig test pits to see what archaeology they could find. They found Roman articles in some gardens in Heath Road, as they were near a Roman Road, as well as crockery and items from later eras across the village.

There are still people living in Hessett who were born here and have not moved from the village.

A coffee morning at the Village Hall after refurbishment in 2016.

St Ethelbert's Church

ST ETHELBERT'S Church is Grade I listed and stands in the shade of yew trees within the churchyard. There are several stone memorials of various types, such as "Table Monument", "Coped" and "Ledger Stones", marking the graves of Hessett folk who died 700 years ago.

Villagers today tell the way of the wind from a 600 year-old weathervane on the church tower, which also has an arrow pointing to heaven, and a sword with a crowned hilt referring to the Anglo-Saxon king, after whom the church is dedicated. It symbolises the story of St Ethelbert, King and Martyr, who was brutally murdered by order of Offa, the pagan King of Mercia in AD 794.

From the churchyard the church is an impressive sight with an ornate parapet running the length of the clerestoried nave. The porch and the tower were built by John Bacon and his wife Isabel. The tower houses five bells singularly sweet in tone, which were originally cast in the 15th Century. Bells one, two and three were recast in 1724 by Robert Midson, John Vacher and John Stephens and bells four and five in 1787 by T. Osborne.

The original church clock probably dated from the 19th Century and was removed in the early 1970s and was looked after by Edward Ashton. It was removed because of the weight of the heavy driving weights which needed a long drop for the weights to work and was causing structural problems to the tower itself.

The clock is now electrical and needs no weights or pendulum. The original clock was returned to the village in 2009 and is inside the church.

Four angels holding shields stand on the parapet of the tower with a row of shields below them bearing the initials 'I' (many years ago 'J's were often written like 'I's) and 'B' thought to be for John Bacon. Under the shields are five carved devices, one represents a swan, the badge of the De Bohun family. There are two possibilities for the swan; one is that the De Bohun family were granted land in Hessett for services to the Crown. The second is that it was placed on the tower to commemorate that it was built during the Abbacy of John Boon, or Bohun who was elected Abbot of Bury in 1454. The fine lofty arch of the tower matches the arcades reaching up to a nave roof, though its angel corbels (usually made in stone or brick) have dwindled.

Isabel (John Bacon's wife), thought to be the sister of the Abbot of Bury, added the south porch with its panelled roof, its three vaulted niches, and in the spandrels of the doorway in which St George and the Dragon appear. John Bacon also built Five Bells Cottage, next to the church, which he left in his Will of 1513 to his sister. A bench just inside the porch bears the mutilated arms of the Bacons, and another has a greyhound, probably their crest.

An inscription in flints along the north side, "Prey for the sowles of John Hoo and Katrynne his wyf, the qweche hath mad y capel aewery deyl. Heytend y westry & batylmentyd y hele" (that is, they had made every bit of the chapel, heightened the vestry and battlemented the aisle). There a 14th Century doorway reveals that John and Katherine Hoo built the chapel in 1492. An inscription in Latin round the 15th Century octagonal font records that it was made in Norwich in 1451, and donated by Robert and Agnes Hoo. The pedestal and bowl is decorated with flowers. New at the same time as the font was the screen with the delicate tracery, in gold, red and other colours which has been painstakingly restored.

Curiously small is the newel staircase to the vanished vaulted rood-loft. Rood is the top of the screen with a cross which has Jesus on (or a crucifix) and at the foot of the cross on either side are Mary and John the Baptist. Rood-loft is a walk way about 4 feet wide in front of the cross. It has holes in the top for candles which are lit from the walk way to be burnt in honour of the statues. The earliest interior fabric of the church is 14th Century and is found in the chancel. This is much as it was 600 years ago, but is darkened now by the organ, which if it could be removed would reveal another lovely chapel with memorial plaques to the Le Heup family. The chancel with its old low seats with wide book rests and a mitred abbot joins a variety of richly carved stalls including a hawk, partridge, viper with the heads of two dragons, doves and pelicans. A sanctuary chair was added in the Jacobean period.

It is unusual to find that a piscina (a stone basin where water used at Mass was poured away) has been carefully renewed, but still retains its mediaeval drain. The vestry floor consists of tiles decorated with lions and roses and also has the remains of a fireplace, with an ancient stepladder to the floor above. A squint hole has been cut through to make a peephole to the altar for use of a recluse or hermit who withdrew from the world for religious reasons and lived in the vestry. The hermit could see the priest's hands holding the sacrament at the altar. A strong door with 14th Century ironwork leads into this vestry.
It is very surprising to find a fuller's club (used for beating cloth in the cloth trade) in a window of the church. The fuller's club is held by one of the boys grouped around St Nicholas, who appears in medieval glass in the south side, and a playing card on its wall. The appearance of a playing card, the six of diamonds, is believed to be the earliest picture of a card in England and dates the painting as late 15th Century.

A wall mural is probably due to the family of Henry Lord Bourchier who held the Manor of Lovaines in Drinkstone and also lands in Hessett. Of special interest is the faded 15th Century wall painting of the seven deadly sins. Pride is at the top and in pairs underneath are Gluttony and Anger, Vanity and Envy, Avarice and Lust. They are presented by two devils which look on as a great tree sprouts from the mouth of hell. Beneath the sins is 'Christ of the Trades' from the 15th Century, about a hundred years after the deadly sins. It shows Christ in the centre and around him a vast array of tools and symbols of various trades.

The walls also have traces of St Barbara holding a tower. There are two other wall paintings. By the north door is the painting of St Christo-

The seven deadly sins wall painting.

pher carrying the Christ-child through the water and at the bottom on either side are two figures believed to be the donors. By the south door is St Michael the Archangel. Crosses were uncovered when the church was decorated but all are fading in daylight.

Another window shows a man with a sword in a purple robe and fur collar, a 15th Century Bishop is in the clerestory and in more old glass in the north aisle is St Nicholas with St James, the Annunciation, and Christ rising from the tomb. The glass in the East window is estimated to date from 1350; other glass seems to date from 1480 to 1500.

Near the gate and close to the path leading to the south porch stands the rare remains of a 15th Century stone cross, from which travelling friars preached the Gospel. These are not so common in this part of the country, but this is one of the largest whole-piece crosses in Suffolk.

We are constantly amazed at the priceless possessions tucked away in our villages, things that any museum must long for; and here is Hessett with two pieces of needlework which are national treasures. Such treasures of Medieval glass, stone and woodwork might seem enough for one village, but something far more precious is a chest made of old chestnut wood with complicated locks and iron bands.

The medieval wooden chest in Hessett Church.

Hessett alone has managed to keep the 16th Century Pyx-cloth (a cloth that covered the chalice cup) and the linen bag, a burse or corporas-case (1400-1430), which was designed to hold the sacramental wafers. The Pyx-cloth is of fine linen over two feet square, and with a hole through which passed the chain on which the Pyx-cloth was suspended above the altar. The cloth is worked to resemble lace. Its silk fringe of rose and yellow has almost worn away, but one of the tasselled gilt balls still hangs from a corner. The burse linen bag is bound with pale green silk and has the holy lamb on one side and on the other a portrait of our Lord and the winged creatures of the Evangelists.

The items are now in the British Museum, but there are framed pictures of them in the church on the wall either side of the font. The village is lucky that Cromwellian despoilers missed this church as all the figures stayed intact. The Access Cambridge Archaeology states that the churchyard contained a never failing spring which supplied part of the village with water, and was covered in 1891. Under the organ is a boiler room, with the entrance on the north side of the church the steps of which have now been filled in. On Saturdays Arthur Harris would light the boiler ready for services on Sundays. If the electric failed Bernard Walmsley would pump the bellows so the organ could be played. Mrs Alice Frost was a church warden and would do the cleaning and look after the Church, which she did for 25 years.

The Union Flag hanging in the church was donated by the Harris family in 1974. Timothy Harris, 21, died following an accident at Portsmouth Dockyard and after the funeral the flag, which had been placed on his coffin during the service, was presented to the family by the naval party. Tim Harris was serving on HMS Hardy.

The Rectors of St Ethelbert's from 1309 to 1999 are listed on the wall inside the church's main door.

	RECTOR	PATRON
1309	Michael de Clare	Abbot of St Edmund
1313	John de Secford	Abbot of St Edmund
1313	Simon de Draughton	Abbot of St Edmund
1317	John de Herwood	Abbot of St Edmund
1322	Alexander Camayle	Abbot of St Edmund
	Alexander Byrd (idem?)	Abbot of St Edmund
1349	Stephen de Tutyngton	Abbot of St Edmund
1359	William de Redenesse	Abbot of St Edmund
1381	Robert Braunche	Richard II
1399	John Boteler	Abbot of St Edmund
14 ?	John Dalanio (Vel Harlstone)	Abbot of St Edmund
1429	John Holym	Abbot of St Edmund
1430	John Calfhawe	Abbot of St Edmund
1436	Edmund Bungey	Abbot of St Edmund
1437	Richard Wyllyam	Abbot of St Edmund
1459	Bartholomew Grey LLB	Abbot of St Edmund
1464	Sir William Chapeleyne	Abbot of St Edmund
1468	Thomas Ballys	Abbot of St Edmund
1476/77	Robert Cracke	Abbot of St Edmund
1523	Thomas Nunne M.A.	Abbot of St Edmund
1548	Edmund Nunne	Edmund Bakon
1561	Thomas Boyton	Elizabeth Bacon
1574	Richard Sadlington	Queen Elizabeth I
1579	Anthony Rowse	Edmund Bacon

1600	Robert Boninge, or Bonynge	Walter Hawghe M.A.
1617	Nathaniel Wicks	
1627	Simon Bradstreete M.A.	Charles I
16 ?	Andrew Chaplyn (Sequestrator)	Parliament – by Arrogation
1662/3	Simon Kendall M.A.	Robert Walpole
1680	Richard Nesting M.A.	Robert Walpole
1724	William Beart B.A.	Thomas le Heup
1740	John Toosey (vel le Tousey)	Michael le Heup
1766	Henry le Heup	Michael le Heup
1778	John Steggall	Michael le Heup
1786	John Steggall	Michael le Heup
1809	Thomas Waddington D.D.	Michael le Heup
1813	Thomas Ellis Rogers	George III
1844	Henry Bunbury Blake	Sir Henry Charles Blake
1873	Richard Morphy M.A.	Charles Stubbs Tinling & John Hannath Marsh
1891	Hannath Michael Blake	Emily Louisa White
1896	Douglas Roper Nunn M.A.	Douglas Roper Nunn, Rector
1904	George Herbert Jones M.A.	Bishop of Ely
1914	Edward Morton Bartlett	Bishop of Ely
1955	Geoffrey Kitson Walton	Bishop of Ely, St Edmundsbury and Ipswich
1961	Eustace Carew MBE, M.A.	Cyril Douglas Edmund Roper-Nunn
1967	George Kenneth Matthew	Cyril Douglas Edmund Roper-Nunn
1974	Denis Bratt	Bishop of St Edmundsbury and Ipswich
1976	Ian Barham	Mrs Valerie Clarke
1980	Anthony David Marsh	(Lord Chancellor)
1986	Roy Rimmer	Memorial of Martyrs of Church of England Trust
1987	Richard Fredrick Webb	Memorial of Martyrs of Church of England Trust
1993	Gerald Harry Clothier	Memorial of Martyrs of Church of England Trust
1997	Anthony Wade Spencer, Assistant Curate	
1999	Nicholas Cutler	Lord Chancellor
1999	Graham Rendle, Ordained Local Minister	

The Rectory

THERE WAS a medieval parsonage, which was in alignment to the church. The first mention of a parsonage is in 1254, the value of the parsonage being £10.

Looking through the Glebe Terriers in 1635 (Ref E14/1/2) the site of the parsonage adjoined the churchyard. The house contained a hall, parlour, kitchen, backhouse, two barns and a stable and a neat house or woodhouse, with an orchard, altogether extending to an estimated one acre. It appears to have been a single storey dwelling as no chambers were mentioned and the family would have slept in the parlour. In 1674 the parsonage had six hearths.

By the 1784 terrier (Ref E14/4/4) the parsonage now has two parlours, three chambers, two garrets and two stables, one of them cut off from an end of one of the barns by a partition. There is a garden, a home stall pasture and the land is still estimated at one acre. The parsonage is lath, cast and tiled. The outhouses are clay, weatherboard and thatched.

In 1813 (Ref E14/4/4) the only addition was a study with garden and barn belonging to the parsonage house on the north side. The parsonage house is timber plastered and tiled. The outhouses are built with timber and boards daubed with clay and thatched. The 1834 terrier (Ref E14/4/4) is exactly the same.

In 1837 the new Rectory was built, where Hessett House now stands, and the old Parsonage was demolished. In 1850 there was the rebuilding of the Rectory and by 1891 the new rectory house had twenty acres of glebe land. In 1912 the value was £200 p.a. and now has 7 acres of glebe land.

In the "The Bury & Norwich Post" – 17th April 1822 the following notice appeared:

**HESSETT PARSONAGE NEAR BURY
TO BE SOLD BY AUCTION BY GEORGE BIDDELL
ON FRIDAY 26th APRIL 1822
UNDER A DISTRESS FOR RENT**

All the Farming Stock, Household Furniture, Dairy and Brewing Utensils, and other Effects; comprising; 2 strong useful cart mares, sow and 10 pigs, road wagon, 2 tumbrills, luggage cart, roll, ploughs, harrows, barn and hand tools, harness &c; bedsteads and furnitures, featherbeds and bedding, chests with drawers, painted clothes press, wainscot writing desk, capital 30 hour clock in case, by Chaplin, mahogany and other tables and chairs, fenders fire-irons, copper boilers, brewing copper; Bath stove, mash and wort tubs, dairy utensils, and other effects; Catalogues of which may be had at the Place of Sale; the Auctioneer's, Bradfield; and White Horse Inn, Beyton.

Sale to begin at Eleven o'clock.

The rectory - now a private house - is behind the village hall. A new rectory was built in 1906 for the Rev. G M D Jones when the church was renovated.

Church Room

IT IS SAID that the church room came from Thurston where Cavendish Hall now stands and was taken down when a new hall was built in remembrance of Mr Cavendish who died when the Titanic liner sank.

There are no records for either Hessett or Thurston that detail anything about the hall being moved, but some time between 1912 and 1913 the church room was brought from Thurston by Ephram Renson who lived in a cottage at the back of Vine Cottage.

According to a Terrier and Inventory of 1924 (Ref FL584/3/6) the church room was built of wood and corrugated iron in the Rectory Paddock. It was purchased and erected by subscriptions, sales of work etc. The Rector, the Rev Bartlett, offered the site on the condition that it be used for any purpose connected with the work of the church and subject to the approval of the Rector.

Reading Room

THE AIMS of a Reading Room were to provide a social and educational meeting place for each community. Richard Morphy who was the Rector at Hessett from 1873 to 1891, described the aims as being mutual society and mutual improvement and abstention for others and, perhaps more attractively, a place of entertainment and to form good fellowships, and to provide the labourers with an alternative to the public house.

The landowner, or committee, provided games and improving literature for the members with tea, coffee and beer which could be purchased. Gambling, fighting and swearing were forbidden and could result in the member being expelled.

Part of the following extract is from the opening of the Culford Reading Room, but of course this could also be a very similar account of the opening of the Hessett Reading Room that was situated in The Street, and set back from the road almost on the present site of the village hall.

"On Saturday night in the presence of a large number of labourers and other working men, the handsome building which henceforth will be known as 'The Reading Room', and which had kindly been erected by the Boy Scouts, but who donated the room is not known, and was for the use of the male inhabitants of the village. No charge will be made for the use of the building."

In 1994 Olive Catchpole recalled:
"The 2nd Troup of Scouts built a hut on to the Reading Room. In the Reading Room the young men used to play billiards and there were newspapers for them to read. Mr Ted Frost kept order in the Reading Room; he lived at Church Cottages, and was the verger and father of Ernie Frost". Olive Catchpole attended Sunday School in the Reading Room, and political parties held meetings and concerts there.

The Mission Hall

From the History of the Bradfield St George Baptist Chapel (Rougham) by J Duncan.

Bradfield St George Chapel (Rougham) built firstly in 1835, secondly 1850, served Bradfield St George, Rougham and Hessett. The population of Hessett in 1844 – 417 and in 1901 – 381.

- Hessett chapel was certified for worship in a house by Bury Baptist Minister in 1841.
- 1823 a house and yard by Bury Wesleyans.
- 1835 a house by John Spink of Beyton. It had a Society on the Wesleyan Plan 1861/6 and 1884/7. John Spink was one of the Foundation Members of Bradfield St George.

Hessett, which comes quite a lot in our history, holds the record as being the only place in the area which had early nonconformist influence in the days before freedom came. The Toleration Act allowed freedom of worship to non-conformists in 1689.

- In the great day of 1662 Andrew Chaplyn was ejected from the Hessett Parish Church.
- 1672 Wm Goodrich certified his own house in Hessett for Presbyterian Worship.
- In 1849 on 11 November David Bland of Hessett was proposed to be baptised. (This was at Bradfield St George Chapel). He was baptised on the 25th November. David Bland was at the Tea Meeting two nights later and it was his proud boast about 66 years later that he had been at every Tea Meeting held by the Church.

- December 17th Bro. John Spink of Hessett fell asleep in Jeasus (SIC). He was not quite 70 years old. His death was rather sudden but peaceful and happy. He had been baptised at Rattlesden and maintained an honourable profession for nearly 40 years.
- 6th January 1850. John Catchpole of Hessett was proposed and was baptised on the 28th.
- 14th April, Wm. Spink of Hessett, son of Bro. Spink, Deceased, was proposed and baptised on 5th May.
- 9th February 1851. It was agreed to have doors to the two seats next to the table pew. Candidates were coming forward from Rougham, Bradfield St. Geo., Beyton, Rushbrook and Hessett.
- 27th April. Special rules were made for the Sunday School. The Brethren, John Last, Henry Frost, and Sister Abi Last of Bradfield St. George with Brother David Bland of Hessett engaged to take the Superintendency.
- 1862. Mr & Mrs Catchpole of Hessett, members of the Methodist Connection, asked permission to be baptised when the pool was open and this was agreed. They do not appear to have joined the Church then but a Marion Catchpole joined in 1864. David Bland was treasurer of Chapel.
- 31st December 1881. Bro G Bird of Hessett died – a member for 37 years, he was one of the original 17.
- March 1890. The committee considered hiring the Mission Hall at Hessett built by Bro. Wm. Bland. The rent was to be £4 a year. Mr Dixon thought the Home Mission would pay the rent.
"The opening services were held on Easter Monday 7th April. Mr Wm. Bland stated that the object in building the Hall was to be an auxiliary to the cause at Bradfield. Mr Dixon preached the following Sunday evening and with two or three exceptions the Mission has been supplied every Sunday evening and well attended as a rule".
- 25th October. Thanks were entered £6 from 'Suffolk and Norfolk' Home Mission for 1½ years rent at Hessett Mission.
- 1893. Easter Monday. 4th Anniversary at Hessett. The Mission Hall was an improvement to the village, so the minutes say and it was formerly an old malting purchased by Bro. Wm. Bland and a part of it made into the present building to seat about 100 people.
The light of the Gospel had been shining for many years in Hessett with Meetings having been held in some ten different places. Forty people took tea at the 5th Anniversary at Hessett.
- 8th April 1901. 8th Anniversary of Hessett, 70 took tea which was superin-

tended by Mr and Mrs Wm. Bland and Mrs Ottley, Bro. Morley provided in the evening when addresses were given.

- 19th April 1897. The 7th Anniversary was held at Hessett. Tea was held in Bro. Wm. Bland's workshop, 105 people attended.
- 1898 Anniversary Tea 80 to 90 present
- 1900 Anniversary Tea 60 to 70 present
- 1901 Anniversary Tea 70 present
- 1904 Anniversary Tea 80 present
- 1906 Anniversary Tea 30 present
- 1907 Anniversary Tea 30 to 40 present
- 1909 Anniversary Tea the smallest they had ever had.
- 1913 Mr Dixon said he felt the services at Hessett could be commenced if our Bro. Mr Melton and Mr Hitchcock could do a Sunday evening one a month.
- 1915, Mrs Beaumont was willing to keep the Mission Hall at Hessett at 6d per week. It was agreed to examine the Mission Hall at Hessett and that an effort be made to purchase it.
- On Wednesday 4th August a Committee was held at the Pastors House re the Mission at Hessett and it was agreed to offer Mrs Wm. Bland £40 for the Hall which was accepted.
Mr D Bland died on April 25th 1917. He had been a shoe maker in Hessett.
- 25th November 1923. The opening of the Mission Hall in Hessett was discussed but held over for a time.
- 20th March 1924. Services were held in connection with the reopening of the Mission at Hessett, there was a public tea.
- 29th January 1925. Re Hessett Mission it was thought desirable to have alternative Sunday meetings at the Mission and at the Chapel.
- 29th November. It was thought desirable to close Hessett Mission during the winter months.
- 6th June 1935. There was a discussion about Hessett Mission and there were to be meetings alternate Sundays the 2nd and 4th of the month.
14th July. Agreed to open Hessett Mission on 11th August.

Family line: Lords of the Manor

FOLLOWING in the family line as far as possible from 1300 to 1782, and with some Wills, I have tried to make a family tree of the Bacon and Le Heup families who were the Lords of the Manor in Hessett.

Cecily Hoo was born in Luton in 1300 and died in Monks Bradfield, now known as Bradfield St George. As far as is possible to tell, the Hoo family originated from Kent. Sir Robert Hoo of Kent was born in 970 and died in the year 1000 in Luton. It was when Cecily Hoo marrying John Bacon II (marked with a *) in 1320 in Hessett that the Bacon family began.

Abbreviations: (b) Baptisms, (m) Marriage, (d) Death

* Cecily Hoo (b) 1300, (d) date unknown (Monks Bradfield)
John de Hoo (b) about 1450, (m) Katherine Tylly (b) about 1454
John de Hoo (b) about 1475, (d) about 1558
Walter Hoo (b) about 1516, (d) about 1587, (m) Agnes Lockwood (b) about 1532
John Hoo (b) about 1552, Jeremy Hoo, John Hoo, Joane (b) about 1558, (m) 1578 Philipe Newgate

John Bacon I, (m) Alice
* John Bacon II, (b) 1299, (m) 1320 Cecily Hoo, (b) 1300
John Bacon III, (b) 1321, (m) 1345 Helena (Gedding ?), (b) 1325
John Bacon IV, (b) 1346, (m) 1371 Helena Tillotts, (b) 1350
John Bacon V, (b) 1376, (d) 1453, (m) 1410 Margery Thorpe, (b) 1390
Sir Edmund Bacon, (b) 1410, (d) 1456 Drinkstone, (m) Elizabeth Crofts, (b) 1415
John Bacon VI, (b) 1430, (d) 1510 Helmingham, (m) 1454 Agnes Cockfield, (b) 1435

George Bacon, (b) 1515, (d) 1569, (m) Margaret Gosnold, (d) 1574
Edmund Bacon, (b) 1554, (d) 1624
Edmund Bacon, (b) 1576, (d) 1617
Edmund Bacon, (b) 1611, (d) 1627
Thomas Bacon, (d) 1635
Henry Bacon, (d) 1651
Lionel Bacon, (d) 1653

Thomas Le Heup, (b) 1666, (d) 1725
Michael Le Heup, (b) 1732, (d) 1792, (m) Merielina, (b) 1734, (d) 1792
Michael William Le Heup, (b) 1756, (d) 1809, (m) Mary Wyche, (b) 1759, (d) 1828
Mary Spring Le Heup, (d) 1785, daughter of Michael William and Mary Le Heup
Merielina Agnes Le Heup, (b) 1791, (d) 1816, daughter of Michael William and Mary Le Heup and wife of Rev. Thos. Ellis Rogers, Rector of Hessett
Ann Le Heup, (b) 1791, (d) 1833, wife of Peter Le Heup
Merielina Agnes Le Heup, (b) 1811, (d) 1837, daughter of Michael Peter and Ann Le Heup, (m) Michael Peter Carpenter.
Michael Peter Le Heup, (b) 1782, (d) 1837, eldest son of Michael and Elizabeth (Nee Gery) Le Heup, both deceased.

The Le Heup memorial in the church.

Personal Wills

Richard Nunne's Will of 1447 leaves a sum of money to the High Altar of St Ethelbert.

Richard Willyam, in 1459, appoints John Bacon an executor of his Will, and mention is made of the Tabernacle of St Ethelbert which he directs to be painted anew at his charges. If the Churchwardens accounts were in existence we would find paid to Robt. Sexton and his fellows for taking down the Tabernacle of St Ethelbert.

Richard Willyam, a Rector of Hessett, was buried in the chancel according to directions given in his Will dated 26th April 1459. He bequeathed XLs (60 shillings - £3) for the reparation of a certain road between Hessett and Bekton (Beyton).

Other Hessett Wills preserved in the Bury Registry show that from 1462 to 1513 there were in Hessett a **John Bacon** the elder, and another John, probably his son. That the Hessett branch of the family was possessed of considerable wealth is evident 60 years later from the Will of **Stephen Bacon**. He unquestionably belonged to the family and in 1444 left lands in Hessett, Rougham and Bradfield Monachorum (probably Bradfield St George) to John his only son.

John Crème's Will of 25th September 1500 bequeathed eight pence (3p) to the bell-man who went about the neighbourhood and rang a hand-bell at every street, before the village cross and upon the Green while chanting a mournful account of the deceased's name. This official asked all who were listening to say a short prayer to God asking for mercy on the soul of the passing. All that evening, and from earliest dawn next day, the church bells tolled a knell.

Thomas Bacon, son of John above, married Ann daughter of Henry Rouse of Dennington in 1513 and died in 1547. Sir Nicholas Bacon, the first Baronet and Lord Keeper of the Great Seal to Elizabeth I, made it his seat and for his descendants. He was born at Drinkstone.

In 1616 **George Bacon** gave the Churchwardens 40 shillings (£2) for the use of the poor and in 1631, Edward Bacon by his last Will and Testament gave the sum of £5 to be distributed annually to the poor people of Hegessett on the first Sunday in Lent.

Simon Bradstreete (SIC), presented by King Charles I in 1627, appears to have borne an infamous character. The Bradstreetes (SIC) were an old Hessett family. Roger Bradstrete (SIC) is mentioned in a deed, preserved in the Parish Chest, and another Roger Bradstrete (SIC) appears in a second deed dated 1586. Simon Bradstrede (SIC) was ejected from the Rectory by Parliament in 1644.

When **Lionel Bacon** died in 1653 without issue the Manor and Advowson then passed to Robert Walpole, the grandson of Lionel Bacon's eldest sister Elizabeth and father of Sir Robert Walpole the first Prime Minister who later became the Earl of Oxford. In the year 1712 Robert Walpole by his last Will and Testament gave £200 to the poor of Hessett, the interest to be distributed yearly.

In 1724 **Aubric Porter** was Lord and Patron, and his nephew John sold the Manor and advowson to Thomas Le Heup. Hessett Hall, the family home, was destroyed by fire and never rebuilt, so the family moved to Bury St Edmunds. The family estate on the death of **Michael Le Heup** in 1809 passed to his two daughters and was in the joint ownership of Mrs Rogers and Mrs Cocksedge.

In 1729 **Thomas Aldrich** left in his Will to Hessett church two silver dishes for use at the Communion Table, and also two pieces of land called Lang-meads for the increase of the Rectory.

In the same year **Roger Parfrey** gave £10 to be paid into the hands of the Churchwardens and Overseers of the Parish, the yearly interest "to be given out to the poor in White-bread upon St Matthew's Day". The sum of £4 was left to the Parish, the interest to be paid annually in groats (worth 4d in old money, or 1½ p today) to the poor widows of Hessett. A piece of land, with a

house and yard was bought by the parishioners for the use of the poor.
From the Coventry Archives is an attested copy of the Will of **Michael Le Heup the Elder** dated 14th December 1748:
To Michael Le Heup (the son) stating all the personal estate of the testator all goods, stock and effects at Hesset (SIC);a large pearl necklace, diamond clasp and large diamond earrings with pearl drops, large rose diamond girdle buckle and gold ring, belonging to the mother, wife and father of the testator, with his father's gold seal with arms engraved on in onyx; the stock in London; 12 silver baffles knives, 12 forms, 12 spoons, 2 salts, 2 upright candlesticks and 1 plate of the same metal.

In 1853 the Manor belonged to Mrs Rogers and Mr C S Tingling; in 1885 it belonged to C T Tinling and Rev. J H Marshall, then in 1896 to Thos. Tinling and Mrs White, and in 1901 to Mrs Tinling and Mrs White.

Most of the Wills prior to 1700 are kept in the Bury St Edmunds Record Office, some are at the Norfolk Record Office (the Norwich Consistory Court – NCC) in Norwich and others are at the National Archives (Prerogative Court of Canterbury – PCC).

The wills and their reference numbers:

1444 Stephen Bacon of Hegesset (R2/9/44)
1447 Nicholas Nunne (R2/9/80)
1474 John Heyward gave XXs (twenty shillings) to the fabric of the Church (R2/10/564)
1492 John Hoo (R2/13/98)
1494 Walter Nunne (R2/13/26)
1500 Robert and Agnes Hoo (R2/15/2)
1500 John Crème of Heggessette (R2/13/193)
1512 Walter Hoo, Yeoman (IC500/46/80)
1519 Robert Hoo of Hegesset (R2/15/2)
1536 John Bacon of Hessett Canterbury (105.1 V) (extc)
1537 Richard Hoo (POOPE 181)
1538 Henry Hoo (POOPE 181)
1540 Harry Hoo (IC500/4/148)
1542 William Hoo (IC500/6/71)
1546 Thomas Bacon, wife Ann, Nicholas Bacon Supervisor of Wills (IC500/129/72)

1548 Robert Bacone, 2nd son of John Bacon, will proved 1500, Canterbury (PCC 11/32)
1553 John Shepard (R2/31/45)
1553 Edmunde Bacon, son of Thomas who died 1546 (A5/4/26)
1553 Agnes Bacon (IC500/28/22)
1557 Stephen Hoo, Husbandman (IC500/20/41)
1566/7 John Bacon of Troston, eldest son of Edmund who died 1553, Canterbury (PCC 11/36)
1570 Elizabeth Bacon, widow Edmund (IC500/1/30/38)
1587 Walter Hoo, Probate: left freehold lands in Hessett, Beighton and Rougham, (IC500/46/80)
1611 George Bacon (PCC 56 WOOD)
1624 Edmund Bacon (AB III 26)
1633 Edmunde Bacon (A5/4/26)
1643 Edmund Hoo (MEADOWE 65)
1670 Henry Bacon (AB IV 118)
1677 Ann(e) Bacon (READ 492)

Population and Census

IN THIS CHAPTER are a range of dates showing the population figures and the main occupations in Hessett. There is a Tithe Map and Apportionment of 1838 showing the owner and occupier of land and buildings in Hessett. The numbers at the side represent where on the map the land was held. The Hearth Tax of 1674 shows how many fireplaces each person had in their houses, also who paid the tax and who were too poor.

The Census was started in 1801 and taken every ten years thereafter, the only time the Census was not taken was in 1941 during the Second World War, although there are not many Census records surviving before 1841. We can find the number of villagers for most of the dates but we cannot look at any Census forms after 1911 as there is a one hundred year closure on them.

In the examples from the Census, key residents have been included, those who made a living doing various occupations and were the heads of households. The rest of the heads of households were agricultural labourers (Ag Lab) and most probably worked on farms in the village. The Census includes the street where people live and lists family members and anyone staying at the address on Census night. When Census day came, the Enumerator would take a form round for the head of the house to fill in details (much as today when the Census is taken). If people could not read or write the Enumerator would fill in the form for them, hence so many different spellings of names.

In the 1841 Census there is very little information given, some of the pages are torn, but it includes where they lived, their name, occupation and whether they were born in the county. By 1901 there was a lot more information including their exact birth place. Most of the children followed in their father's footsteps when going to work. The father may have been an agricultural labourer and all the sons of working age also worked on farms. When the family was in need of money some of the children who should have been at school were out at work, bringing in a meagre wage. Of the farms listed in this Census only Malting Farm, Elm Farm, Valley Farm and The Shrubbery are now being farmed.

I have enclosed only two census records; the population for 1841 was 417 and in 1901 it was 381. These show how occupations have started to change, although the farmers are more or less the same.

The two Kelly's Directories, of 1904 and 1937, show the occupations of people in the village and the District Valuer's Field Book lists the properties with the occupant and landowner.

Population living in Hessett

The population between 1800 and 1980
(276 – 487) varies by about 200 people.

1801	323	1911	382
1811	343	1921	342
1821	393	1931	311
1831	428	1941	not taken
1841	417	1951	285
1851	487	1961	276
1861	454	1971	329
1871	437	1981	381
1881	428		
1891	353		
1901	381		

Hearth Tax - 1674

The Hearth Tax was been introduced by Charles II in 1662 and a charge of two shillings (10p) levied per hearth per year. As there were 97 hearths in Hessett, in 1674 the sum of £9.14 shillings (£9.70) was raised from the village. Out of interest, there were some 60,000 hearths in Suffolk at this time. The Bill was rescinded in 1689 when King William III came to the throne.

Hessett - number of hearths in the property

Mr Oldredge	18	Thomas Howe	
Robert Hunt		Mr. Goodrich	3
George Mickfield	2	Richard Chinery	5
Jos. Durrant		Phill. Mothersole	2
Fra. Miles	2	Mr. Springe	6
William Johnson		Ja. Bammocke	
Henry Fuller	4	Thomas Bell	3
An. Barly		Thomas Crowe	
Edmund Barly	3	William Motham	3
Jo. Tebbet Jun.	2	William Barly	
Mr Kendall, Clerk	6	Jo. Grandum	5
Jo. Tebbet snr.	6	William Sussimis	
Bar. Parker		Edward Shipp	4
William Collen	5	Widow Paufry	3
Jo. Bulbrooke		Sam. Nutt	
Thomas Pissy	4	Thomas Barly	4
Miss Colman	4	Jo. Bruce	
Richard Durrant	5	TOTAL	97

CERTIFIED – (No tax to pay) - too poor

Thomas Barret		Ri. Howes	2
William Randall	3	James Carter	
Widow Rust		Thomas Jermin	2
Robert Hunt	3	Thomas Debnam	
Widow Cricke		Widow Rowe	2
Widow Johnson		Jo. Bixley/Jo. Blawes	2
Widow Clarke	2	Clergyman	
Jo. Balaam		Simon Kendall	6

Tithe Map and Apportionment of 1838
(T80/112).

The Tithe Commutation Act was brought before Parliament in 1836. A Tithe is a tenth part of agricultural or other produce, personal income, or profits contributed either voluntarily or as a tax for the support of the church or clergy or for charitable purposes.

No on Estate Map		Owner
95	Elms Farm	Robert Alderton
97	Houses	
313	Rans Green	
43	Bells Inn	
39	Cottage and Garden	Natanial Nottley and William Cocksedge
37	House, yards and gardens	James Green
36	Cottage and gardens	James Last and Benjamin Cocksedge
35	Cottage and garden	Landowner – Overseers of the poor – Thomas Rosse and others
34	Town Piece	William Canham – Trustees of Town Estate
33	Garden	Edward Wilkin
32	Maltings	William Canham
31	Cottage and garden	Thomas Barker
30	Cottage and gardens	Peter Walliker, William Herrington, William Presling
29	Cottage and garden	Robert Burrows
1	Old Hall Garden	Michael Peter le Heup
2	Hall Orchard	Michael Peter le Heup
3	Hog Yard Meadow	Michael Peter le Heup
4	Hall Orchard	Michael Peter le Heup
11	Homestall and part of Orchard	Michael Peter le Heup
308	Cottage and garden	James Ottley and Henry Makings
302	Cottages, yards and gardens	John Manning, Robert Steggall, John Cocksedge, William Austin, John Sutton, John Steggall
301	Cottage, yards and gardens	William Nice and James Cocksedge

300	Cottage and garden	John Bland, Will Bland, John Bland Junior
299	Cottage and yard	Alice Gooday
294	Moat Wood	Michael Peter le Heup
297	Cottage and gardens	Robert Aldridge and Thomas Hubbard
289	Cottage, garden and orchard	Thomas Brooks
288	Farm, homestall and garden	Henry Green
103	Parsonage, homestall garden	Rev. William Steggall
109	House, Malting offices, homestall	John Gooch
111	Green Meadow	Henry Green
119	Cottage and garden	James Clarke and Ann Eaves
120	Farm house and homestall	Thomas Newport
175	Farm house and homestall	Jemima Bauly
123	Farm, homestall and orchard	Henry Green
124	Pighsle	William Canham
125	Farm, homestall, house and garden	William Canham (also owner) James Alderton and George Hubbard
169	House and gardens	James Boggis
255	Woodhall Farm, Homestall and Rookery	Ephraim Taylor
237	Free Croft Barn, yard, etc	William Walpole
220	Stonhams (Valley Farm)	James Nunn

1841 Census - Hessett population 417

Address	Name		Age
Hicket Heath	Joel Raker	Farmer	45
Freecroft Farm	Samuel Robinson	Farmer	40
	Amelia Raker	Farmer	60
Great Green	Jemima Bauly	Farmer	65
Great Green	Henry Groom	Farmer	35
Great Green	William Canham	Farmer	45
Elms Farm	Robert Alderton	Farmer	30

Agricultural Labourers	67	Carrier	1
Bailiff	1	Cooper	1
Blacksmith	2	Cordwainer	1
Cabinet Maker Apprentice	1	Female Servant	8
Carpenter	4	Gamekeepers	1

Gardener	2	Pensioner	1
Independent	2	Publican	1
Male Servant	3	School Mistress	1
Malster	1	Shepherd	1
Mason	1	Shoemaker	4
Parish Clerk	1	Shoemaker Apprentice	1
Pauper	2	Woodman	2

1901 Census - Hessett population 381

Address	Name	Age		Employment
The Rectory	Douglas Nunn	Priest	42	
Shrubbery Farm	James P Bauly	Farmer	50	Employer
Thorington Farm	John Batham	Farmer	30	Employer
Green Farm	Arthur Howlett	Farmer	29	Employer
Spring Farm	Frederic Squirrell	Farmer	33	Employer
The Green	William Hubbard	Farmer and builder	46	Employer
Freewood Farm	John Squirrell	Farmer	57	Employer
Malting Farm	Joseph Liffen	Farmer	88	Employer
The Street	Thomas Robinson	Farmer	37	Employer

Agricultural Labourer	59	Mat Maker	1
Assist School Mistress	1	Nurse	2
Baptist Minister	1	Plate Layer G.E.R.	1
Brewery Clerk	1	Plowman	1
Carpenter	3	Railway Labourer	1
Carpenter & Joiner	1	Retired Bankers Clerk	1
Carrier	2	Retired School Master	1
Engine Driver	1	Road Man	1
Game Keeper	2	Seamstress	1
Gen/House/Farm Serv	8	Shepherd	1
Grocer and Baker	1	Shoemaker	1
Grocer	1	Shop Assist	1
Grocers Labourer	1	Stockman	1
Horseman	12	Tailoress	1
House Keeper	3	Thatchers Labourer	1
Hurdle Maker	1	Timber Merchants Clerk	1
Independent	1	Tree Feller	1
Inn Keeper	1	Woodman	4
Journeyman Baker	1	Yard Lad	1
Laundress	6	Yard Man	4

Kelly's Directory 1904

Listed in the Directory of 1904, when the Hessett population was 381, are: Mrs Tinling and Mrs White, owners of the Manor and principal landowners; the trustees of the late Frederick Nunn, Walter Thomas Walpole, John Hargreaves and Frederick Squirrell Esq. who are also landowners; Robert Beckford Govey; the Rev George Herbert Daniel Jones M.A and William Jordan.

Commercial

Daniel Alderton – Farmer

John Batrum – Farmer

James Philip Bauly - Shrubbery Farm – Farmer, Hessett and at Felsham

Arthur Howlett – Farmer

George Nunn – Farmer

Henry John Raker - Great Green – Farmer, insurance agent and agent for Prentices Manures, King & Son's Seeds, Alliance Assurance Co and Railway Passengers' Assurance Co & C

Frederick Squirrell - Spring Farm – Farmer and Miller (steam)

John Squirrell - Freecroft Farm – Farmer

Thomas Walter Walpole – Farmer

William Hubbard - Hill Farm – Farmer, Wheelwright, Blacksmith

Mahershalalhashbaz Sturgeon – Parish Clerk

William Bland – Carpenter

Arthur Sturgeon – Carpenter

Herbert Bruce – Shopkeeper

Miss Susannah Bruce – Shopkeeper, Post Office

Henry Hubbard - Five Bells Public House Keeper

William Lambert – Hoop & Hurdle Maker

James Last – Shoemaker

Thos. Riches – Cocoanut & Wool Mat Maker

White Field House, Drinkstone - Thomas Woodruff – Farm Bailiff to John Jewers Esq

William Sturgeon – Carriers to Bury, Wednesday and Saturday

Albert E Moore – School Master

District Valuer's Field Book
(IL501/1/14) c. 1910

Maps, sometimes known as the Lloyd George Domesday survey, were produced as a result of the 1910 Finance Act and were accompanied by a Field Book listing the owner and occupier of each property; the address or a description of the property; the extent of the property (measured in acres, roods and perches) and its valuation, together with other financial information. Unfortunately, the map for Hessett has not survived but information can be found in the field book.

Building	Occupier	Owner
Free Wood	J Squirrell	G W Agnew
House and shop	Miss Bruce	J Elvier
House, building and land	Squirrell Land,occupier	Self owner
Valley Farm	H Nunn	Nunns Trustees
Lands at Drinkstone Park	J Bauley	J Hargraves
Shrubbery and Heath Farms	J Bauley	J Hargraves
Malting Farm and part		
Heath Farm	J H Raker	Tingling and White
Late Bricklayers Arms		
– cottage	T Austin	Mrs Salvage
Five Bells	Mrs Hubbard	Tingling and White
House and shop	H Bruce	W Thompson
House and shop	Wm Hubbard	Self owner
House, Land, Buildings	Wm Hubbard	Tingling & White
House and shop	W Winter	Self owner
Hessett House	Major Topham	Self owner
School House		School Trustees
Stone Pitt	J Bauley	J Hargraves
Rectory	Rev. E M Bartlett	Self owner
House, Land and Buildings	D Alderton	Tingling & White
House and Land	Wm Bland	Self owner
Land at Valley Farm	J Jewers	Hargraves Est
House, Land and Buildings	J Jewers	Hargraves Est
House and Land	J Squirrell	Walpole Trustees
House and Land	J Battram	Self owner
Cottage R Govey	D Bland	
Rectory and garden	Rev G H D Jones	Self owner

Kelly's Directory 1937

The Kelly's Directory of 1937, when the population of Hessett was 311, lists Major J C Hargreaves as a landowner, the Rev. Edward Bartlett was the Rector and Lt-Col. Thomas Topham lived at Hessett House.

Commercial

Major Agnew – Freewood Farm – Farmer

Jas. Barton – Freecroft Farm – Farmer

Arthur Bauly – Malting and Elm Farm – Farmer

Sarah Bauly – Shrubbery Farm – Farmer and Landowner

Samuel Rogers – New Farm – Farmer

Frederick Squirrell – Spring Farm – Farmer

Jas. Bidwell – Hurdle Maker

Charles Bland – Vine Cottage – Boot and Shoemaker

Herbt. Bruce – Shopkeeper and Post Office

Alex Renson – Shopkeeper, Sweets

W & G Mills – Grocers, Bakers, Confectioners, Pork Butchers and Hardware Dealers

Samuel Ernest Garrod – Five Bells Public House

Lawton Halls – Wheelwright

Herbert Sturgeon – Carpenter

The village at war

FOLLOWING the assassination of Archduke Franz Ferdinand of Austria, heir apparent of Franz Josef I, and his consort, the Countess Sophie, in Sarajevo, Bosnia on 28th June 1914, a series of inter-related events resulted in the invasion of Belgium by four German armies on 4th August. Their objective was to conquer France by conducting surprise attacks through that neutral country. England declared war on Germany on Tuesday 4th August 1914.

Britain was committed, by treaty, to defend Belgium and the British Expeditionary Force (BEF) of about 110,000 men moved to France where they confronted the German Army on 22nd August in positions along the Mons-Conde canal, just inside the Belgium border. The Germans were stopped in their tracks by rapid rifle fire but with far greater strength and out-flanking movements the German armies forced the BEF to retire the following day. The French Fifth Army was already in full retreat and the BEF was forced to fight a number of holding actions, including the costly battle of Le Cateau, in an effort to check the German progress south.

The German advance continued but was finally checked early in September, close to Paris, in the Battle of the River Marne involving the BEF, and the French Fourth, Fifth, Sixth and Ninth armies. The Germans retreated on 8th September and then attempted to hold the line at the River Aisne, but by the end of the month a stalemate had developed. Both sides attempted outflanking manoeuvres that later became known as the "race to the sea". By the time the Belgian coast had been reached at Nieuport, a continuous line of battle stretched from the North Sea to Switzerland. Less than twelve weeks after the first shots had been fired, the war of movement was over and for the next four years troops were engaged in trench warfare along the Western Front. At the outset the strength of the British Regular Army stood at around 235,000 men, of which almost half were serving overseas, usually in India. The units stationed in the UK formed the BEF of six divisions and one cavalry division. There were also fourteen divisions in the Territorial Forces supported by fourteen mounted brigades, each trained to a high standard and organised much the same as the Regular Army. However, their role was intended for home defence and a Territorial could not be required to perform overseas duties. The majority did, of course, subsequently volunteer to serve abroad and the fine record of the Territorial Force is a matter of history.

An ex-soldier who was on the reserve list at the commencement of the war was immediately recalled to colours. Lord Kitchener, on appointment as Secretary of State for War, recognised the need to increase the size of the British Forces without delay and asked Parliament to authorise an additional 500,000 men. He embarked on his famous recruiting drive "YOUR KING AND COUNTRY NEED YOU. A CALL TO ARMS".

Many men enlisted, being told "it will all be over by Christmas", and some thought of it as an adventure and excitement as well as a chance to go overseas, many for the first time.

By the end of 1914, the strength of the British Forces stood at 720,000 and by July 1916, despite the high losses, the strength, including Commonwealth Volunteers, was 1,420,000.

At the end of the war the total sacrifice was calculated at over one million British and Commonwealth dead. The French and German losses were far higher. One attempt to give reality to these figures is to imagine a continuous column of a million men marching four abreast past the Cenotaph. As the head of the column reached the Cenotaph the last four men would be in Durham. It would take the full column three and a half days to march past the Cenotaph.

In the cemeteries of the Great War, a cross of sacrifice, varying in size according to the number of graves, would be sited in cemeteries with forty or more graves and a stone of remembrance would be included in cemeteries with four hundred or more graves.

The wording on the stone of remembrance, "THEIR NAME LIVETH FOR EVERMORE", was chosen by Rudyard Kipling from the scripture, "Their bodies are buried in peace, but their name liveth for evermore". Kipling is also responsible for the wording, "KNOWN UNTO GOD", that appears on all headstones marking the graves of those unidentified by name.

Headstones are two feet eight inches high and of a standard design representing equality in death whatever a man's rank or religion. Atop the stone is usually an emblem depicting the badge of the regiment or service for British Forces or the country emblem. Below this are the service or regimental number (omitted for officers), the rank, initials, surname and British decorations. Then below is the date of death and age, if known.

The "Battlefield Cemetery" includes those where men are buried in the ground where they fought and died. Burials took place fairly soon after death and were often in large shell holes or even trenches. These cemeteries tend to be relatively small and will often include men of the same battalion. There were hundreds of such cemeteries at the end of the war, but the majority were moved as the process of constructing cemeteries was rationalized.

"Comrades Cemeteries" are those that will be found just behind what was the front line, usually located alongside a farm track, a country lane or behind a front line village. Soldiers killed during trench duty were buried by their colleagues, others who had been injured and then died in forward dressing stations were also buried in these cemeteries. "Communal Cemeteries" take their name from the French Commune and refers to those local civilian cemeteries that were used in some areas to bury soldiers before military cemeteries were established.

Further back from the front line are the "Medical Unit Cemeteries" that were located close to main dressing stations and casualty clearing stations. These were often near railway lines offering transport for when soldiers were fit to travel. Other examples can be found close to where large base hospitals had been set up near the channel ports.

"Concentration Cemeteries" are those developed by the War Graves Commission where it was necessary to provide new burial places for thousands of bodies as it was not possible to leave the many small burial areas that were scattered across what had been the battlefield. Most of the men buried in these cemeteries will have died on the immediate surrounding battlefield.

There are nearly one thousand Commonwealth War Grave Cemeteries in France and Belgium with no less than 600,000 headstones. There are also 18 memorials listing the names of those who died but have no known grave.

At The National Archives at Kew, the records of the First World War are now stored. They were housed in the docks area of London for many years and during World War II a lot of the records were destroyed during air raids. Some records were rescued but a lot were burnt or have water damage.

When the archives were examined the records for Hessett men William Henry Hubbard of the Royal Navy, George Stiff and Ernest G Bullett of the Suffolk Regiment were the only ones to be found.

The information on the other soldiers has come from the disc of "Soldiers who died in the Great War" and from the local newspaper "The Bury and Norwich Post". From a book at the Bury Record Office called "The History of the Suffolk Regiment" brief notes have been taken to give an idea of how the troops travelled around during the time of the war.

The records for World War II were only allowed to be looked at in 2015 as there was a 75 year closure on them. There is a cenotaph for the Suffolk Regiment in St Mary's Church, Bury St Edmunds.

The First World War Memorial in the churchyard of St Ethelbert's Church in Hessett is one of the largest whole piece crosses in Suffolk, and was designed by the then rector, the Rev. Bartlett.

The Hessett men who died in WWI

William Henry Hubbard

William was baptised on 17th July 1887. In the 1901 Census he was 13 and his parents were Henry and Kate Annie Hubbard who were the innkeepers of the Five Bells. William Hubbard died on 22nd September 1914, aged 27, lost at sea on HMS Cressy in the North Sea (as inscribed on his parents stone in the churchyard).

HMS Cressy was an armoured cruiser built around 1900. The vessel was on patrol with HMS Hogue and HMS Aboukir and was sighted by a Submarine U9. The U-boat torpedoed HMS Aboukir which was sunk. HMS Hogue, who was picking up survivors, was also sunk by U9.

HMS Cressy had picked up survivors and was underway, and had seen the submarine U9 and attempted to ram, but failed. Cressy was damaged by a torpedo, and then hit by a second torpedo whereby she sank. 837 men were eventually rescued but 1459 personnel died.

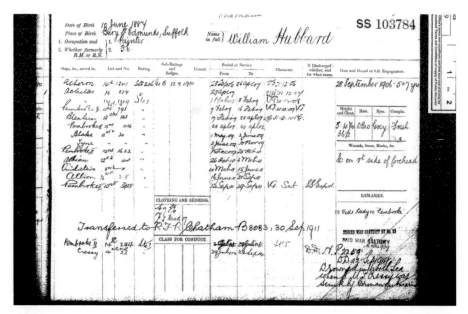

The service record of William Hubbard who died in September 1914

Pte Herbert Green

Herbert was a private, No.23743, and served with the 9th Battalion in the Suffolk Regiment. He died of wounds on the 22nd September 1915 aged 19 in Flanders, France. Herbert Green was born 7th April 1896 and was baptised 29th November 1896, and in the 1901 Census Herbert was aged 5 and the seventh child of Jacob and Elizabeth Green and living in The Street.

In the newspaper, "The Post", 6th October 1916 is an article: "With regret we have to report the death of Pte Herbert Green, 9th Suffolk Regiment, 4th son of the late Mr Jacob Green and of Mrs Green, of the Old Hall, Hessett". Pte Green, who was 19 years of age, joined the colours in January, and was drafted to France some 3 months later. A letter from the sister in charge of No. 5 Casualty Clearing Station states that the deceased was suffering from severe wounds in the back, and "although everything possible was done for him, he died". The cemetery in which he is buried is Corbie Communal Cemetery Extension, and is on Plot 2, Row E, Grave 31.

Pte George Stiff

George was a private, No. 2326, and served with the 5th Battalion in the Suffolk Regiment. He was killed in action 21st August 1915, aged 20, in Gallipoli, and is named on the Helles Memorial, and is on Panel 46 and 47. In the 1901 Census George was aged 6 and the son of George and Annie Stiff living at Butchers Farm, Rattlesden.

Pte Stanley William Gladwell

Stanley was a private, No. 3/8087, and served with the 2nd Battalion in the Suffolk Regiment. He was killed in action on 20th July 1916, aged 21, in Flanders, France, and is named on the Thiepval Memorial, and is on Pier and Face 1C and 2A.

L/Cpl Ernest Catchpole

Ernest was a Lance Corporal, No. 201461, and served with the 4th Battalion of the Suffolk Regiment and was killed in action 26th September 1917, in Flanders, France, and is named on the Tyne Cot Memorial, and is on Panel 40 to 41 and 162 to 162A.

Ernest was baptised on 30th May 1892 and is the son of John and Isabella Catchpole. In the newspaper "The Post" of Friday 2nd November 1917 it reports:

> The sad news has reached the relatives of L/Cpl E Catchpole, 14th Suffolk Regiment that he has been killed in action in France. The appended letter gives some details regarding his unfortunate and sad death:
>
> **4th Battalion Suffolk Regiment, B.E.F.**
> **30th September 1917**
>
> *Dear Mr Catchpole, I very much regret to inform you of the death, killed in action on 26th September of your brother Ernest, No 201461 LC Corpl Catchpole. He was killed by a shell as he was advancing to the attack with his Lewis Gun team. I shall miss him very much, for I have known him now for many months, and he has always done most gallant work in the company. He was previously one of my company stretcher bearers, and I have always found him working most gallantly under difficult circumstances. Personally, and on behalf of all my company, I offer you sincere sympathy in your sad loss.*
>
> *Yours Sincerely,*
> Harold Pretty Capt. O & A Company 14th Suffolk Regiment.
>
> The late L/Cpl Catchpole joined the colours on 1st April 1916 and had been in France 14 months. He was expected home on leave very shortly, but alas his sad fate prevented this. Before joining the colours he had resided with Mr and Mrs D Bullett, Green Farm, Hessett for six years. The deepest sympathy is felt for his relatives.

Pte Walter Green

Walter was a private, No. 24449, he served in the 2nd Battalion with the Suffolk Regiment. He died of wounds 25th April 1918, aged 26 in Flanders, France. The cemetery where he is buried is Tournai Communal Cemetery Allied Extension. In the 1901 Census Walter Green was aged nine and was baptised on the 10th July 1892, the fifth child of Jacob and Elizabeth Green living in Hessett.

Pte Harry Bullett

Harry was a private, No. G/15089, and he served in the 9th Battalion with the Royal Sussex Regiment. He was killed in action 4th November 1918, aged 30. He is buried in the Cross Roads Cemetery, Fontaine-au-Bois, 1.F.12.

Harry Bullett was baptised 9th September 1888 the child of Elizabeth Bullett and in the 1901 Census he was aged 13 and was living on The Heath, the grandson of Charles and Mary Bullett.

Pte Alfred Benningfield

Alfred was a private, No. 425509. He enlisted at Bury St Edmunds into the Manchester Regiment, 2nd/5th Battalion Army Service Corps and was transferred to No 425509, 254th Company, Labour Corps attached 542nd Company and died 31st October 1918, in Flanders, France. In the 1901 Census he was aged eight and the son of Arthur and Elizabeth Benningfield from Beck Row, Mildenhall.

William Borley's grave in Hessett churchyard.

Pte Bertie Bullett

Bertie was a private, No. 40087, and served with the Hertfordshire Regiment. He was killed in action on 9th October 1918, aged 25, in Flanders, France. He is buried at Naves Communal Cemetery Extension 11.D.16. He enlisted at Warley, Essex and was formerly No. 3855 of the Essex Regiment. Bertie George Bullett was baptised on 4th June 1893 in Hessett. In the 1901 Census Bertie is aged eight, living at the Old Hall and the grandson to William Bullett.

Pte Bertram Cocksedge

Bertram, No. 18400, served with the 9th Battalion in the Norfolk Regiment and was killed in action 18th September 1918, Flanders, France, and is named on the Vis-en-Artois memorial, Panel 4. He was born in Rougham, and in the 1901 Census Bertram was 13 and the son of George and Emily Cocksedge living in Kingshall Street, Rougham.

Pte Charles John Prentice

Charles, No. 4300, served with 15th (The Kings) Hussars – Household Cavalry and Cavalry of the Line (inc Yeomanry and Imperial Camel Corps). He was killed in action 8th August 1918, aged 28, Flanders, France, and is named on the Vis-en-Artois Memorial, Panel 3. In The Post newspaper of 30th March 1919, the Roll of Honour for Beyton mentions Pte Charles Prentice:

> "Killed in Action – Pt Charles Prentice, the husband of Mrs Prentice of Hessett, and third son of Mr H & Mrs Prentice of Brakly Close, Gt Barton fell in action on 8th August at Harbonniers, France. Pte Prentice was a reservist on the outbreak of war. He had nearly completed 12 years' service in the Kings Hussars and had been in France for 4 years. He leaves a widow and one boy".

Pte Ernest George Bullett

Ernest was a private, No. 50121, and he served with the 8th Battalion in the Suffolk Regiment. He was killed in action 6th May 1917, aged 23, and is named on the Arras Memorial, Bay 4. In the 1901 Census Ernest was seven years old and the grandson of George and Amelia Bullett living in Spring Cottage. He was the husband of Ethel Mary Bullett, nee Catchpole of Brockford Green, Stowmarket.

There are two War Graves Commission graves and headstones in Hessett churchyard for William Borley and John Whiting.

Bdr William James Borley

William was a private, No. 59872, and joined the 3rd Battalion Northampton Regiment. The 3rd Battalion was a recruiting and training unit for other battalions and its men did not serve overseas. It moved to Portland, Dorset, then to Gillingham in Kent and Scrapsgate on the Isle of Sheppey in May 1918 and remained there until the end of the war.

William died at the Sheerness military hospital on 15th November 1918, four days after the end of the war, aged 30. The cause of death was given as influenza, which killed millions worldwide. William was baptised 1898 the seventh child of Charles and Eliza Borley. He was the husband of Ella Priscilla Green.

John Whiting

John Whiting, number 13942, served with the 8th Battalion in the Suffolk Regiment, and died of wounds on 7th August 1916, aged 21, at Fulham Military Hospital. He had been brought back to England after being wounded at the Battle of the Somme. In the 1901 Census John is aged six and son of Emily and grandson of Elijah and Eliza Catchpole living at the Old House, Hessett. He was baptised in 1895.

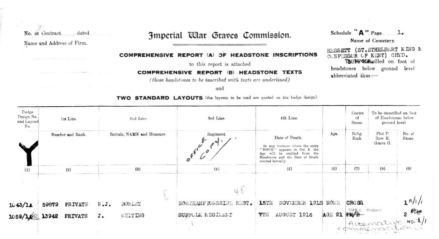

The War Graves Commission order for the Hessett gravestones.

Roll of honour

The men of the village who gave their lives in the First World War are on the previous pages. Those who served in World War 11 are named on the Roll of Honour in the church with includes those of the First World War who have a red cross next to their names. As far as we know, the men of World War 11 all came home.

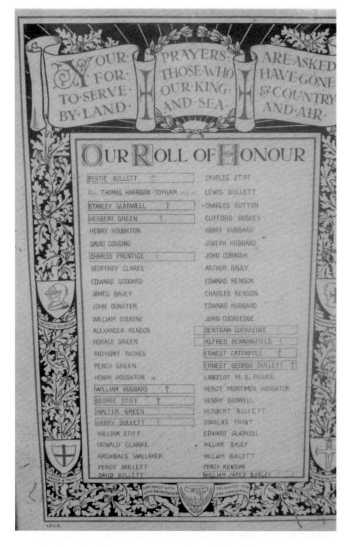

Col Thomas Harrison-Topham
Arthur Bauly
James Bauly
William Bauly
Henry Bidwell
Lancelot M S Bruce
David Bullett
Lewis Bullett
Herbert Bullett
Percy Bullett
William Bullett
Clifford Bussey
Geoffrey Clarke
Oswald Clarke
John Cocksedge
John Cornish
David Cousins
William Cousins
John Dunster
Douglas Frost
Edward Gladwell
Edward Goddard
Horage Green
Percy Green
Henry Houghton
Henry Houghton Jnr
Percy Houghton
Edward Hubbard
Harry Hubbard
Joseph Hubbard
Alexander Renson
Charles Renson
Edward Renson
Percy Renson
Anthony Riches
Charles Stiff
William Stiff
Charles Sutton
Archibald Wallaker

Suffolk Regiment action WW1

2nd Battalion Suffolk Regiment

January – August 1914, *Ireland at Curragh – The Ulster Crises*
Arrives in France: The advance into Belgium.
August 1914, *France and Flanders*
First contact with the enemy. Retreat from Mons via Dolorosa.
August – September 1914, *France*
The battle of Le Cateau.
September – December 1914, *France*
Advance to the Aisne: Battle of the Marne. Passage to the Petit Morin and the Marne: Battle of the Aisne, at La Bassee. Towards Ypres: Battalion spends Christmas 1914 in Belgium.
January 1915 – April 1915, *Flanders*
In the Vierstraat area, trench warfare. The Flanders Front: trench foot.
April – June 1915, *Flanders*
From Vierstraat to the Salient.
June – September 1915, *Flanders*
First attack on Bellewaarde; the Suffolk man a rare fighter and digger. Sanctuary Wood; the Ypres ramparts; Hooge.
September 1915 – June 1916, *Flanders*
Second attack on Bellewaarde. Counter attack on September 30th; Divisional rest at Eecke. Back to the Salient; The Bluff and its capture: St Eloi, Vierstraat and Kemmel. In the HGQ area.
July 1916 – July 1917, *France*
Arrive on the Somme at Les Celestins: Battle of Bazentin and Delville Wood. A quiet front in the Loos sector. Back to the Somme: Ancre, or the battle of Serre. To Arras: The Wellington Caves.
April 1917 – March 1918, *France*
Battle of Arras 1917. First battle of the Scarpe. Unsuccessful attack on Guemappe. Second attack of the Scarpe and Arleu. Infantry Hill. Transferred to a quiet sector. Ypres once more: Polygon Wood. Farewell to the Salient. Back to Wancourt: Guemappe sector.
July – November 1918, *France*
The Hinges sector: the advance to Victory. Second Battle of the Somme 1918. Albert 1918. Capture of Gomiecourt. Attack at Exoust St Mein.

Breaking of the Hindenburg Line. Battle of Canal du Nord. Second battle of Le Cateau. Battle of Selle.

November 1918
Battalion marches into Germany. Reincarnated in England. Back to Ireland. Unveiling of the Le Cateau Memorial. Battalion goes to China.

4th Battalion Suffolk Regiment

July – December 1914, *Home and France*
Territorial Army enters the line of Battle. Battalion training in England. Joined the Jullandur Brigade at Vieille Chapelle. Defence of Givenchy 1914. Christmas behind Bethune.

January – April 1915, *France*
Neuve Chapelle.

April – May 1915, *France*
In the Salient with the Lahore Division. Battle of St Julien. Battalion returns to the Neuve Chapelle area.

May – September 1915, *France*
Battle of Aubers Ridge. Attack at Rue du Bois. In the Neuve Chapelle area. Peaceful September.

September 1915 – July 1916, *France*
At Neuve Chapelle. The Jullundur Brigade supports an attack on Mauquissart. 4th Battalion joins 15th Division at Verquin. Christmas at Rainbert. Battalion transferred to 33rd Division: raids. Battalion is hurried down to the Somme.

July 1916 – April 1917, *France*
Bazentin: 4th Battalion supports attack on High Wood. Pozieres: attack on 18th August; allowed a short rest. Christmas in the trenches near Rancourt. Advance to the Hindenburg Line.

April – March 1918, *France*
Arras 1917. Hindenburg tunnel. Second battle of the Scarpe. The great struggle for Guemappe. Battalion goes to Flanders. Four months in the Salient; third battle for Ypres. Battle of Polygon Wood.

March – June 1918, *France*
German offensive in Picardy. Battle of St Quentin. Battle of the Ancre 1918. The actions of Villers Bretonneux. Digging trenches the Albert/Amiens Road.

August – November 1918, *France*
Advance into Picardy and Battle of Amiens. Breaking of the Hindenburg Line. An unfortunate night air-raid. Battle of Epehy.

November 1918, *France and home*
Battalion spends another Christmas in France. Joins the Army of Occupation in Germany. Return to Ipswich.

5th Battalion Suffolk Regiment

1915, *Gallipoli*
Sailed for Egypt; land in Gallipoli; Suvla Bay. The evacuation battalion sails for Egypt.
January 1916 – December 1917, *Egypt and Palestine*
The Sinai Peninsula. Invasion of Palestine. First and Second battles of Gaza. Storming of El Arish redoubt. Third battle of Gaza. Battle of Nebi Samwil. Capture of Jerusalem.
December 1917 – November 1918, *Palestine and Syria*
Captures Bornat Hill. A cheerless Christmas. Actions of Tel Asur order and counter order at Ludd. The final offensive. Battle of Megiddo. Storming of Observation Hill. Collapse of the Turkish Armies. Battalion reaches Haifa. Armistice with Turkey. Beirut. Armistice with Germany.
November 1918, *Egypt and Home*
Arrives Beirut. Most arrived home July 1919.

9th Battalion Suffolk Regiment

September 1914 – September 1915, *Home and France*
Battalion raised at Shoreham. Joins 24th Division. Lands in France. Towards Loos.
September 1915 – July 1916, *France*
Battalion at Loos. Battalion in the Ypres Salient. Battalion goes to Albert Sector.
August 1916 – April 1917, *France*
Mailly-Maillet Wood. In front of the Quadrilateral. Battle of Flers. Courcelette. Battle of Morval and Transloy. Resting in Annezin. Christmas in army reserves at Noeux-Les-Mines. Prolonged stay in the Loos-Hulluch sector.
April 1917 – February 1918, *France*
Loos-Hulluch sector. Raids and counter raids. The Cambrai operations. Christmas at Bailleulmont. 9th Battalion receives order for disbandment. Disbanded at Courcelles-Le-Comte.

Telephone Exchange

MRS CAMPION, who lived in the Thatched Cottage, Beyton, operated the first Telephone Exchange. It then moved into Bury Road to a house next to a shop which was on the corner of Church Road and was then run by Mrs Rouse whose husband ran a garage in Bury Road.

When automation arrived the exchange moved further along the road into the exchange which is still there today.

These are the Hessett telephone numbers as listed in Kelly's Directory for 1933/37.

Rev. Edward Morton Bartlett, Rectory, Hessett	03
Lt Col Topham, Hessett House	11
Wm Mills & Goodwin, Shopkeepers	12
Herbert Bruce, Shopkeeper & P.O.	19
Frederick Squirrell, Spring Farm	46
Arthur Bauly, Malting & Elm Farms	58
Herbert Bruce, Shopkeeper & P.O.	66

The numbers for Hessett were also included with the numbers for Beyton and Rougham, hence the large gaps in between the numbers. Later the figure 2 was added before the number so that 03, 11, 12 etc became 203, 211, 212.

A little learning: Hessett School

THE PLANS FOR the building of a school in Hessett were put forward on 15th May 1847. The site chosen was where Flint Cottage and The Old School house are now, called Ran's Green. When the school was built it was designed for 65 children with an average attendance of 44.

In 1841, according to the Census, Mary Holby was the School Mistress and was living in The Street. The school was erected on Ran's Green in 1848 with a residence for the master and was surrounded by a garden and playground. The master and mistress received a joint salary of £45 a year. By 1851 there was a school master whose name was Thomas Spooner and his wife Alice Spooner who was the National School Mistress.

In "A Survey of Suffolk Parish History" by W Goult there is mention of a Dames School in 1818, where children were sent while their parents were working in the fields. This could have been the Dames School at Vipers Hall. There have been several schools in Hessett:
1818 Dames School

Hessett School around the 1900s.

1833 Daily School – 32 attended (reference: Suffolk Parish History)
1847 Public Elementary School, for 78 pupils (ref: Kelly's Directory 1916)
1874 the National School Mistress: Miss Jemima Dorling (ref: 1871 Census)
1891 National School - 50 attended (ref: Suffolk Parish History)
1904 Albert E Moore was School Master
1912 average attendance was 63 (ref: Suffolk Parish History)
1925 Mrs C J Farley was School Mistress

The school closed in about 1957 and most of the children went to Drinkstone Primary School, with the older children going to Beyton Secondary School.

Mr John Welton's mother was the teacher of a private school. Mrs Welton lived next to the Police Station at Rougham and cycled to the school every day. The school opened in 1939, firstly at The Poplars in Quaker Lane, then in 1944 it moved to The Old Rectory, Beyton. It moved to The Shrubbery, Hessett in 1947-48 and when the school closed all the children, about nine years of age, went to various private schools such as Culford School and Moreton Hall School. These are some of the pupils who attended the school: John Fairbrother, Raymond Rogers, Martin Bauly, Leslie Halliday, Brigett Halliday, Margaret Daniels, Ann Walton, Ann Mitcham, Brian Mitcham, Nigel Renson and Clive Jewers.

Hessett School 1926
Back row: Ethel Cornish, Ivy Cocksedge, Olive Sutton, Annie Cornish, Dorothy Gibson, Ethel Gibson.
Middle: Victor Cocksedge, Lloyd Cocksedge, Thomas Cocksedge, William Bullett, George Bullett, Alfred Bullett, Florence Cocksedge.
Front: Cyril Sutton, Leslie Sutton, Margaret Cundy, ? Cundy, Reginald Cornish, Peter Cornish, Vera Bullett, Arthur Bullett, Jack Cocksedge, Joseph Cundy.

One for the road: The Five Bells

THE PUBLIC HOUSE is a Grade II listed building, possibly 13th, 16th and 17th Century and built in about five phases. It has one storey and attics, a two storey cross-wing, a hall range to left, a cross-wing at the centre, and an addition to the right. It is timber framed and plastered, with pantiled roofs, the roof beams are the original rafters, and there are two gabled 19th Century dormers with small pane windows.

The two central red brick chimneys are 17th Century, both with rebuilt upper shafts. The hall was rebuilt during the 17th Century with a butt-purlin roof, but reusing a good mid-16th Century first floor structure, with a massive binding beam and floor joists of large section, an open fireplace with deep cambered lintel. The right hand range was added in the 17th /18th Century.

The oldest part seems to be in the kitchen where there were wooden shutter runners, which are no longer there. Sheds to the right of the inn had a fence with double gates with a bike shed in front on which was a board with the

timetable for the buses going to town. The gents' toilet was outside to the right hand side as you face the inn at the back. There was a rail in front of the inn for people to tie up their horses and in the middle shed were horse troughs which are still there.

Printed in "The Post" of Friday March 14th 1930 is an article about the Five Bells when Mr S E Garrod was the landlord.

"The title of the public house the Five Bells is derived from the Five Bells hanging in the church tower just across the road, and it is quite customary to name the village public house after this."

Little is known of the history of the inn; it is a low, tiled house, in the centre of the front façade rises a gable, which is supported at its base by old carved brackets. The chimneys on the roof being very plain give no clue to the date of the house.

To the left of the building is the bar, a low room of great age, almost the whole wall on one side of this room consists of a huge fireplace. The floor is composed of irregular red tiles and the low ceiling has heavy beams.

Taken from 'The Post,' Friday 14th March 1930.

"The Bells once did its own brewing up until 1910. In the 1930s the Bells was not a tied house and it is thought that before long it would be bought by an East Anglian brewery."

We are not sure when the pub became under Greene King but it must have been in the 1930s.

Pub landlords

1753	William Swann	1856	James Waylett
1806	Robert Groom	1873	William Aldridge
1835	W Howard/H Humphrey	1879	Mrs W Aldridge
1838	William Howard	1883	William Hubbard
1844	James Lawrence	1888	Henry Hubbard

1908	Mrs Kate Hubbard	2002	John & Kim Muir
1916	Henry Houghton	2007	Various Managers
1925	Robert Mizen	2010	Louise Anthony
1929	Saml. Ernest Garrod	2012	Closed
1937	Gertie Eleanor Garrod	2012	Reopened – Alli Clarke
1954	Dennis Stafford Metcalf	2014	Closed
1968	Vera & Fred Stebbing	2015	Reopened – Deborah and
1971	Anthony Ernest Pywell		Frank Hazell
1976	Anthony Finningham	2016	Closed
1979	Neil David Reginald Parrin	2016	Reopened
1984	Denis Leon Symis	2017	Closed
1998	Andrew & Eileen Leggett		

In 2016/17 the pub was sold by Greene King. The new owners are building a house in part of the pub garden and renovating the pub.

Five Bells inn sign

The Grade 11 listed pillar is an old brick pier, late 17th Century or early 18th Century, and was said to be the survivor of a set of four once standing at the entrance gateway to a drive to Hessett Hall (demolished 18th Century). However, on a map of 1723 (Ref E3/22/2.18) or on the OS map of 1904 (Ref

45.14) there is no sign of a drive to The Hall.

The brick pier had been used for the inn sign for the Five Bells and is constructed of red brick patterning with burnt headers on each face. It is about 0.6m square, and 4m high. The plinth is about 1.5m high, with moulded brick cornice and weathered offset. At the head is a further cornice and a flat lead capping. A wrought iron frame with scrolled crown supported the sign. There are a few of these sign posts now standing in England.

Regulars at the Five Bells in the 1890s.

Beer House

Mrs Olive Catchpole remembers the beer house:

> There was a pub on the Heath (where Well Cottage and Bridge Cottage are now) and they were alongside of the two rows of thatched cottages, one of which was burnt down.

> The pub has had several names, The King William, The Gun and also The Bricklayers Arms.

> Well Cottage and Bridge Cottage were originally one house, the pub being in Well Cottage and a skittle ally in a shed in the garden of Bridge Cottage. This was pulled down in the 1950s.

> There was also a pub at the fork of Smallwood Green called The Rag and Louse and The One Bell.

Hard times

SINCE THE MIDDLE AGES various wealthy people and charities have provided for poor people in Hessett. From the Will of Walter Nunne dated 10th January 1494 (Ref 1c500/2/13/26) it states:
"and geve at the seyd yerday yerly 13d unto the pore pepylle and also the seyd William and his eyrs and his succesors wchult uphold and kepe the almesse hous in the seyd lands".

Also in the Will of John Bacon, dated 1510 (Norwich Registery), he leaves to his sister Margaret Fuller:
"3 almesse housys bi the churchyard, to be kept in repair. After Margaret's discease her son Thomas will always repair, bylde and kepe up the saide almes houses."

When the Poor Law Act was passed in 1601 it was to help people who were elderly, ill, unemployed, unmarried mothers and children abandoned and if anyone had sickness, were unable to work, or if villagers fell on hard times the church and the elected overseer would provide for them with money collected as 'poor rates' from the richer families of the village. The overseer's post was created about 1572 and they were elected annually. They provided food, clothing and fuel for anyone in need. People who were travellers and in need of help were usually sent back to their own village.

In 1692 a further Poor Law Act required account books to be kept with half-yearly accounts signed by the parish overseers and witnessed by the church-warden. With the General Workhouse Act of 1723, the parish could set up a 'workhouse', where if you were unemployed you could be set to work. If you refused to work it meant no relief or housing. In 1729 the Hessett Terrier (Ref 806/1/77) states that "there are two houses adjoining to the churchyard inhabited by such poor persons, as cannot pay rent".

Under agreements such as deeds of feoffment (a medieval legal arrangement which transferred rights of ownership of land), several pieces of land were given to the village.These gifts included a deed of feoffment from 1498 for 'Gyldehall Yerde' (Guildhall Yard), three roods of land (a rood was equal to a quarter of an acre) which was enclosed by a ditch and was planted with fruit trees. A house called the Guildhall stood on the land. Another piece of land, "Town Mead", a field off Manor Road towards Felsham (Ref T80/1,2 plot 201), was given to the village. It was two acres but no use was specified.

Another deed dated 20th September 1716 was for the piece of land called Hinderclay field, which may or may not have been a piece of land which was planted as a grove on the 1838 map. There are two groves, one called Great Hinderclay Grove (plot 207) and the other Little Hinderclay Grove (plot 143), but no Hinderclay Field, (Ref T80/1,2) consisting of two acres.

The piece of pasture ground called the Guildhall yard was half an acre. A piece of land called Churchfield is a field at the back of the church from Back Lane, which ran along side Elm Farm, (Ref T80/1,2 plot 92) containing 3 roods, a meadow of 2 acres, and the Close of wood called Cloits, is a field on the east boundary towards Drinkstone (Ref T80/1,2 plot 141) were assigned to one body of feoffees to be used for the relief of the inhabitants of Hessett (Ref Suffolk Archaeology Vol IV page 324).

The Poor and Town Estate held under deeds of a very ancient date were used in trust partly for the poor, and partly for the common benefit of the parish. Under the Enclosure Act, Cloits and the Town Mead were given in exchange for an allotment on Hicket Heath.

From "The Charities in the County of Suffolk, London 1840" book it states: "Sir Jeffery Burwell's charity for the parish of Rougham was laid out under the direction of the Court of Chancery in 1726 in the purchase of £135-10s-10d (£135.54) Old South Sea annuities, standing together with a further sum of £200 belonging to the Parish of Hessett."

From the "Bury and Norwich Post" newspaper of 28th March 1787 is an advert for:
"Wanted at Easter a person to take charge of the Workhouse and the Poor of the Parish, for particulars apply to the Church Wardens and Overseers – A good character is expected".

The following year on 27th February is another advert where applicants need to apply to the parish overseers: "Wanted a proper person to undertake care of a Workhouse, in the Parish of Hessett in Suffolk".

The Guildhall yard, by now called the Workhouse yard, became the workhouse and consisted of nine tenements. The cottages were situated where the house Red Tiles house now stands, next to Guildhall Cottage. They were occupied rent-free by poor families and the land let for £16.6s.6d a year; of which £1 was paid to the Parish Clerk, with £4.19s being distributed among the poor. Under the Poor Law Act £8 was paid annually to the Board towards the support of the sick and aged; 17s.4d to the widows, the remainder was applied in the service of the church.

In 1770 (Ref 806/1/77) a Glebe Terrier refers to "one alms house and small piece of land abutting East on the churchyard". In 1794 a later Glebe Terrier states: "Two cottage houses and yard adjoining, about half an acre in the occupation of Thomas Jacob, abutting East on Hessett Street the two cottages here mentioned are now made into a workhouse".

Guildhall Cottage about the turn of the 20th Century.

On Wednesday 24th October 1804 the "Bury and Norwich Post" reported:
"At the last quarter sessions James Sutton, a pauper in the poor house
of Hessett, was convicted of an assault upon the Governor of the said
workhouse and sentenced to be imprisoned for a fortnight in the House
of Correction."

In 1805 the position became available and within three weeks of placing the
advert, the position had been filled with the appointment of Robert Dowsing.

Then in 1834 the Old Poor Law changed from parish to Union System of poor
relief. Again in the Hessett Terrier (Ref E14/4/4) it records that "four cottage
houses and yard adjoining about half an acre, in the occupation of William
Canham, abutting East on Hessett Street; the cottages here mentioned are now
made into a workhouse".

The Bury & Norwich Post & East Anglian – 4th November 1835 records:
The first meeting of the Board of Guardians of Stow Union was held at
the poorhouse in Onehouse on Monday night when John Edgar Rust Esq,
was unanimously elected President, and John H Heigham Esq, Vice President; Mr Marriout Clerk of the Court; Messrs Oaks, Bevan and Co and
Mr Hart, Treasurers, Dr Kay auditor of accounts. The meeting was
attended by H Wilson Esq, M.P, J E Rust Esq, J H Heigham Esq, The
Revds Anderson, Green and Phear and among the following Guardians
elected was William Canham of Hessett.

The houses were sold sometime between 1855 and 1895.

In White's Directory of 1855 it states: land consists of the Guildhall and four
Cottages occupied rent-free by poor families. The union is divided into three
districts with a surgeon at a salary of £100 a year and a relieving officer at
£90 a year; for each district. The election of these and other officers will take
place on the 10th November next. Dr Kay gave an able exposition of the plan
to be adopted in administering the Poor Laws with the Union which appeared
to give general satisfactory and the thanks of the meeting were unanimously
voted to him.

On the 17th April 1919, Henry Houghton and Simon Green are overseers to
the poor.

Law and order

THERE HAS ALWAYS been stealing, poaching and "getting your own back". Suffolk was divided into four quarter sessions. The court for Hessett sat at Bury St Edmunds which was in the Liberty of St Edmund, an area comprising the eight 'hundreds' – the administrative areas – which made up West Suffolk. It was called a 'liberty' as the Abbey at Bury had complete legal jurisdiction and could collect taxes, rather than the money go to the crown. Hessett was in the Thedwastre hundred.

Petty quarter sessions were held four times a year, and mainly led to transportation. The Assizes, if a Judge was needed, sat twice a year. Only a Judge could don the black cap and sentence death, which was sparingly used.

In 1328 Alexander Byrd of Hegesete was accused of being part of one of the lawless mobs who destroyed the buildings and other property belonging to the Abbey. He was fortunate to have been able to clear himself and to have been pronounced innocent.

Late in the 16th Century John Hales and his wife Margaret, being vagrant beggars aged about 35, on the 3rd August (year unknown), but in the reign of King James (1603 – 1625), were whipped at Hessett, according to the law for wandering and had to get to Sheppridge in the county of Cambridge in six days.

Under the 1601 Poor Law, men who fathered children but did not marry the mother, or were caught stealing, poaching or arson would be sent to the house of correction for six months, where they were whipped when they arrived, during their sentence and before they left prison. They would spend most of the day on a tread mill or in a cell on their own turning a handle, which after every circle of the handle it would bring up a number, and they would have a certain amount of numbers to show they had done their work. If longer than six months they were put into prison while awaiting trial, then sent to either a hulk or straight for transportation if a ship was leaving. The prisoners were often held in hulks in the middle of rivers or out at sea, just off the coast before being moved, which could have been up to four years.

In 1820, under The Home Secretary, Sir Robert Peel, a lot of death sentences were downgraded to transportation. If they were given the death sentence they were only in prison three days before being hung.

On 5th July, 1836 James Parish from Hessett was convicted at Suffolk quarter sessions in Bury St Edmunds. He was sentenced to be transported for life for stealing two lambs the property of Hessett farmer R Alderton. He sailed on the ship "Lloyds" on the 25th March 1837 along with 200 other convicts to New South Wales, Australia, and arrived on 17th July 1837.

People convicted of crime which was not considered serious enough for hanging, but were found to have been in trouble before or found to be troublesome, were transported to America between 1711 and 1775. After the British were evicted from America they had to look at alternative places for holding prisoners. As there was nowhere to send the prisoners from 1776 until 1787 they were kept on hulks in rivers or at sea. From 1787 up until 1868 they were transported to Australia. Firstly they went to New South Wales, from 1788 to 1840, and also to Van Diemen's Land, now Tasmania, from 1803 to 1853 and finally Western Australia from 1850 to 1868. After the transportation ceased larger prisons were built in England.

In 1580 there was a House of Correction, established by the Feoffees of Bury in Master Andrews Street, now Bridewell Lane. The prison moved and was on the corner of Woolhall Street and the Buttermarket. In 1626 the Feoffees purchased Moyse's Hall for the town goal, house of correction and workhouse. A new workhouse, goal and house of correction remained until 1805. This was closed when a new prison was built in Sicklesmere Road which was opened in 1805 and closed in 1877. Offenders were then sent to Ipswich Prison which closed in 1920 and now they are taken to Norwich.

Looking through the Bury St Edmunds Gaol books for the years 1844 to 1873 there were 30 men from Hessett convicted of various crimes, some being convicted two or three times during these years. The offences were poaching; stealing beans, peas, turnips, fowls, eggs, wheat, a drinking glass, coal, a bearing van, boots, and clothes; disorderly conduct, malicious damage, payment of bastardy, assault, molesting and coercing, and misbehaviour in the workhouse. They received between seven days hard labour to nine calendar months hard labour; two were discharged and two were fined.

Out of the men convicted one person had four convictions, three were convicted twice, the remainder were convicted once. There were also ten women convicted, charged with stealing clothes, eggs, beans, boots, acorns, jewellery, and a toilet cover, receiving clothes, assault and malicious damage. Their sentences ranged from three days hard labour to six months hard labour. Only one women was convicted twice, the rest once. (Ref Q/AGrl to Q/AGr13)

Hessett people convicted 1844-1873

15th May 1844, **Robert Cocksedge**, Labourer, aged 14. Offence against the game laws at Hessett. Fined 20s, costs 22s. Prison: one calendar month.

15th May 1844, **Isaac Cocksedge**, Labourer, aged 17. Offence against the game laws at Hessett. Fine 20s, costs 22s. Prison: one calendar month.

20th January 1845, **William Goshawk**, Labourer, aged 30. Offence against the game laws in the night time at Rougham. Prison: 6 weeks and fined.

26th February 1845, **Alfred Green**, Labourer, aged 20, single, father John Green. Offence against the game laws at Hessett. Prison: 14 days.

7th October 1845, **Issac Cocksedge**, Labourer, aged 18, single, father William Cocksedge. Offence against game laws at Drinkstone. Prison: 3 months, once before for poaching.

8th October 1845, **Alfred Green**, Labourer, aged 20, single, father John Green. Offence against game laws at Drinkstone. Prison: 3 months, once before for poaching.

13th May 1846, **Issac Cocksedge**, Labourer, aged 18, father William Cocksedge. Offence against the game laws at Drinkstone. Fined £5, costs 16s. Prison: 3 calendar months hard labour, twice before for poaching.

20th April 1847, **Issac Cocksedge**, Labourer, aged 20, single, father William Cocksedge. Charged with felony. 14 Days, three times before for treachery.

14th December 1847, **Benjamin Roe**, Labourer, aged 18, single (residing in the Stow Union House) but a native of Hessett, father William Roe. Misbehaviour in the workhouse by refusing to work with others. Prison:14 days.

7th January 1863, **Charles Sturgeon**, Labourer, aged 20. Killing a partridge at Hessett. Three calendar month's hard labour.

9th October 1863, **James Cocksedge**, Labourer, aged 29. Disorderly conduct at Beyton. Prison: 1 calendar month hard labour.

9th October 1863, **William Mothersole**, Labourer, aged 33. Disorderly conduct at Beyton. One calendar month hard labour.

10th August 1864, **Sophia Spink**, born Rougham, aged 47, father dead, widow. Stealing ½ peck of Windsor beans at Hessett. Prison: 14 days hard labour.

18th August 1864, **Sarah Cocksedge**, servant, aged 23, single, father Edward Cocksedge, labourer, Stow Union. Stealing a pair of boots at Bury St Edmunds. Prison: 2 months hard labour.

3rd October 1964, **Frederick Harrington**, born Hessett, living Rattlesdon, Labourerr, aged 21, father John Harrington, gamekeeper, Rattlesdon. Using a net for the purpose of poaching at Rattlesdon. Prison: 1 calendar month hard labour.

7th November 1864, **Robert Frost**, vagrant, aged 65, father dead. Stealing turnips at Bury St Edmunds. Prison: 1 month hard labour.

21st December 1864, **Modiah Bullett,** Labourer, aged 19, father Edward Bullett, labourer, Hessett. Disorderly conduct at Hessett. Prison:7 days.

1st August 1866, **Sarah Goshawk**, aged 20, single, father William Goshawk, labourer, Hessett. Malicious damage at Drinkstone. Prison: 7 days hard labour.

31st October 1866, **Robert Green**, married, aged 45. Stealing 12 fowls at Hessett. Prison: 21 days hard labour.

7th November 1866, **Abraham Nunn**, married, aged 35, father George Nunn, Labourer, Hessett. Stealing 12 live fowls at Hessett. Discharged on exam.

7th November 1866, **Abraham Frost**, Labourer, single, aged 32, father John Frost, Labourer, Hessett. Stealing 12 live fowls at Hessett. Discharged on exam.

13th February 1867, **George Aldridge**, cooper, aged 29, father Robt Aldridge, labourer, Hessett. Non-payment of orders of bastardy at Tostock. Prison:1 calendar month.

21st March 1867, **Zachariah Scarfe**, Labourer, aged 52, widower. Stealing 8 hens eggs at Hessett. Prison: 2 months hard labour.

21st March 1867, **Emily Scarfe**, servant, aged 19, single. Stealing 8 hens eggs at Hessett. Prison: 1 month hard labour.

21st August 1867, **William Green,** born Hessett, living Bradfield, Labourer, single, aged 59. Stealing a bearing van at Clare. Prison: 14 days hard labour.

2nd October 1868, **Sarah Goshawk and child (9 months)**, single, aged 22, father William Goshawk, labourer. Assault at Hessett. Prison: 7 days hard labour.

28th October 1868, **Arthur Sturgeon**, carpenter, aged 35, married. Stealing wheat at Rougham. Prison: 6 calendar months hard labour.

30th November 1870, **Mary Ann Goodwin**, Rougham, born Hessett, Labourer's wife, aged 26, father William Goshawk, labourer. Stealing acorns at Rougham. Prison: 3 days hard labour.

4th April 1871, **Robert Browning**, blacksmith, aged 21, father Frederick Browning, blacksmith. Assault at Bury St Edmunds. Prison:14 days hard labour.

21st June 1871, **Maria Manning**, servant, aged 16, father Frederick Manning, labourer, Hessett. Stealing a silver watch guard, one pair of gold earrings, one silver knife and other articles at Nowton. Prison: 21 days hard labour.

30th March 1872, **George Oldrick**, cooper, aged 34, went to school in Hessett for 6 years, married with 2 children aged 8 and 3. Assault in Bury St Edmunds. Sentence 2 months hard labour, unless paying £2-7s-6d (paid same day).

8th July 1872, **Susannah Green**, Labourer's wife, aged 45, went to school in Hessett for 7 years, married with 7 children ages 22 to 8. Stealing one green plaid dress and black silk handkerchiefs at Bury St Edmunds. Prison: 4 months hard labour.

8th July 1872, **Ellen Cocksedge** and child, Labourer's wife, aged 22, father Robert Green, labourer, Hessett, went to Hessett school for 5 years, married with 3 children. Stealing a print dress and various articles, at Bury St Edmunds, 6 calico chemises and other articles at Bury St Edmunds. One day hard labour and 6 months hard labour.

8th July 1872, **Emily Cobbold**, Labourer's wife, aged 40, father Henry Cocksedge, Labourer, Tivetshall, went to Hessett School for 2 years, married with 3 children. Receiving 6 calico chemises and other articles knowing them to be stolen at Bury St Edmunds. Prison: 6 calendar months hard labour.

11th September 1872, **William Roberts**, hoopmaker, aged 48, married 8 children. Stealing peas from a field at Hessett. Prison: 14 days hard labour.

19th February 1873, **William Cooke**, Labourer, born Hessett, living Bradfield St George, aged 19, single. Stealing an overcoat at Hessett. Prison: 1 calendar month hard labour.

4th June 1873, **Amos Green**, Labourer, aged 33, married with 6 children. Stealing a drinking glass at Bradfield St George. Prison: 7 days hard labour.

28 July 1873, **Louisa Peck**, Norton, born Hessett, aged 50, married, 4 children. Stealing a toilet cover at Norton. Prison: 10 days hard labour.

13th January 1874, **Arthur Sturgeon**, Carpenter, aged 39, married with 8 children. Stealing a quantity of coals at Hessett. Prison: 9 calendar months hard labour.

11th June 1874, **Albert Nunn**, Labourer , aged 21, went to Hessett school for 3 years, father Henry Nunn, labourer. Molesting and coercing one Edward Howlett at Hessett. Prison: 1 calendar month hard labour.

Zachariah Scarfe, Labourer, aged 59, widower with 5 children. Stealing ½ peck of bean meal of the value of ninepence at Hessett. Prison – 4 calendar month hard labour.

Recreation

THE BOY SCOUTS HUT was a tin hut at the top of Hubbards Lane beyond Valentines Way, where houses were built in the 1980s. There have always been buildings beyond the newer houses in Hubbards Lane and there was also a pond here. Mr Godden was the Scout Master who was assisted by his wife, and the house they lived in was named Thorington Farm but later renamed Thorington House.

The 1st Hessett Scouts in 1928. Back row, John Cocksedge, Charles Mills, Leslie Sutton, Arthur Sturgeon, Mrs Godden; middle row, Will Bullett, Sidney Sturgeon and Fred Sturgeon; sitting, Mr Godden, George Bullett, Victor Cocksedge, Thomas Cocksedge and Reginald Sturgeon.

The Scouts then moved to a room added to the side of the Church Room, as the article from the Free Press and Post of Saturday July 30th 1932 states: "The 1st Hessett Scout Troup opened the new headquarters. It was opened by the Suffolk County Commissioner for Boy Scouts, Rear-Admiral W. D, Paton, the room is a substantial building adjacent to the Church Room."

The village hall was bought from Thurston by Ephram Renson, but it cannot be exactly stated where in Thurston the hall was removed from. It is believed to be the old Cavendish Hall. The old Church Room was taken down and the new village hall was built and opened, according to a plaque in the hall, by Gertrude Sturgeon from Hessett and Florence Bamford from Beyton on 4th December 1982.

In a field to the right of Shrubbery Farm the village played their football and cricket. When that field was put down to crops they moved to a field at the back of the farmhouse.

At the Five Bells the bar games of quoits, dominos and darts were played. From the Bury Free Press & Post in 1932 are three reports about the Scouts, one is a Christmas party, also about raising money for a new Scout hut.

Hessett Football Club in the 1924-25 season. Back row, Gerald Mills, Victor Clements, William Bauly, Frank Harris, Charles Frost, Sidney Hubbard (landlord at the Five Bells), Frank Bauly and Herbert Bullett; front row, John Frost, Sidney Ling, Lewis Clark, Ernest Frost and William Bussey.

The Five Bells quoits team with the Woolpit League Cup 1935-38. Back row, George Osborne, Albert Gant, Frank Harris and Charlie Green; front row Horace Green, Charles Frost (captain) and Philip Friston.

In the Bury and Norwich Post, January 8th 1909, is an article about a play called "The Enchanted Glen". It was arranged by the Miss Jones sisters and was performed by children in the schoolroom.

A play called "Everyday in Fairyland" was performed at the Five Bells in February 1977. It was written and directed by Mr Shackerley Bennett. The cast were Tony Fillingham, Nikki Shackerley Bennett, Caroline Williamson, Mike Williamson, Ron Ayres, Brian Jones, Sue Harris, and Eileen Whiting. After the play a Revue came about a month later with nine acts being performed by players with about 80 people cramming themselves into the pub.

There was also an article in the Bury and Norwich Post on 9th August 1941 of a drawing match, which is ploughing a straight line with horses and a tractor.

In the 1960 and 70's a Ladies Club was formed. The ladies held their meetings in the village hall, with many of the local ladies from Hessett and Beyton attending. The Ladies Club was formed by the rector's wife Mrs Marsh and was originally held in the Rectory at Beyton. When the Church Room was ready they moved up to Hessett. The meetings were held once a month with speakers and also outings organised.

In March 1976 the team of darts players took part in a match at Ixworth Greyhound against Rattlesden Rising Sun. Unfortunately they lost 7 to 23 in the 9-a-side semi final.

Farms and farming

Elm Farmhouse

ELM FARM was part of Drinkstone Park and as there is only one farmhouse in Drinkstone Road it could have been called Link Farm (Ref FL651/13/4). It is a Grade II listed building. In the 1400s it was a hall house and in the 17th Century, two storeys were added. It is timber framed and plastered, with a concrete tiled roof, which was once thatched.

It has a central early or mid-15th Century chimney of red brick, which is an inglenook fireplace with a bread oven which has been there about 600 years. It had a sunk date panel in the base, now missing, and a saw tooth (having serrations like a saw) shaft. There's a doorway at lobby entrance position, early 19th Century columns and ornamental brackets under a cornice, and a 20th Century door with two vertical panels.

This advert appeared in the Bury Post in September 1920:

On Tuesday, September 28th at 12.30 o'clock
The Elm Farm, Hessett
(in conjunction with Messrs, Woodward and Woodward)
The Live and Dead Farming Stock
by direction of John R Hargreaves, Esq.

From deeds and records held by the family, Mr Arthur Philip Bauly rented Elm Farm in 1896 prior to purchasing it in 1929, when he then appealed for a rent reduction. In 1953 major repairs were undertaken at Elm Farm in September of that year.

Mr Albert Gill, who was a builder and decorator and living where Bramble Lodge is now, built the wall at the front at Elm Farm.

Elm Farmhouse, Drinkstone Road, Hessett.

New Farm

NEW FARM was built as a Council Farm and was erected in 1913 with 30 acres of land. Samuel Rogers took over the running of the farm in 1914 and in 1948 his son bought the farm and ran it.

Samuel later lived in Quaker Farmhouse in Quaker Lane, Beyton. He built the first house on the left in Quaker Lane and named it New House when he moved in. The farmhouse was let to the horseman and the cowman while they worked for the farm. The rest of the family lived in Hessett.

Samuel's grandson Ray lived at Sunrays next to New Farm in Hessett.

Valley Farm

VALLEY FARM, on Hessett's southern boundary with Felsham, was originally a single storey. There has been a building on the land since the 13th century. Valley Farm was enlarged and renovated under instructions of Frederick Nunn in his will of 1872 (Ref: HD557/1064/2).

The farm was then called Hessett Valley Farm and is a timber framed building with wattle and daub walls and a thatched roof. There are Tudor bricks in one of the fireplaces which is an inglenook.

The Bury & Norwich Post & East Anglian of 9th September 1835 reported:

AT HESSETT, HOLE FARM

Near Felsham
On Tuesday, October 6th at Eleven O'clock

The entire and excellent farming stock (including dairy of very prime milch cowes, reared upon the premises), nearly new agricultural implements, dairy and brewing utensils, household furniture &c of Mr Abraham Bacon, whose lease expires at Michaelmas.

On the map of 1838, Valley Farm was called Hessett Hole, one assumes because of the dip in the landscape. In the 1851 Census, Hole Farm was occupied by James Calver farming 125 acres.

At the back of the farm in 1851 was a cottage which was called Hole Cottage where Morris Bird lived. He was an agricultural labourer who probably worked on the farm. Between the Census of 1861 and 1871 Hole Farm had changed its name to Valley Farm and was occupied by Isabella Groom farming 200 acres.

Hole Cottage had also changed its name to Hole Farm Cottage. Hole Farm Cottage has now gone but Valley Farm is still a working farm.

Spring Farm

THE HOUSE on Manor Road today known as Spring Farm was previously called Homestall Farm and Manor Farm. In 1838 the landowner at Homestall Farm was William Groom and the farm was occupied by Henry Groom, who on the 1841 Census is recorded as being aged 35 and a farmer.

In the mid-1800s, the timber-framed Homestall Farm burned down, but no record can be found of the exact date. It was rebuilt in about 1850 using Woolpit White bricks for the front wall and red bricks for the rest of the building.

At the turn of the century, Frederick Squirrell (aged 33 on the 1901 Census) was the farmer at Spring Farm. In the 1904 Kelly's Directory, Frederick Squirrell is described as a farmer and miller who milled by steam. Before there was a mill in Hessett, village farmers had taken their corn to Beyton Mill. The steam-driven mill at Spring Farm was removed in the 1980s.

Frederick's daughter Dorothy Squirrell married James Edward Bauly from nearby Shrubbery Farm in 1920. In 1956 James (Jimmy) Bauly took over Spring Farm and farmed there until his death in 1984. Dorothy died in 1965. Spring Farm was left to Jimmy's daughter, Mrs Kathleen Bayer. The house fell into disrepair but has now been renovated and is a family home.

Thorington Farm

THORINGTON FARM and farmhouse were at the top of Hubbards Lane on the left hand fork, round what is now Valentines Way, and facing the fields.

There has been a building on this site as shown on the 1838 Ordnance Survey Map and in 1891 John Bruce was a farm servant and in 1901 John Batham is the farmer. There was also a Mr and Mrs Boon who farmed there and many years later it was lived in by Mr and Mrs Maskey and then called Thorington House.

In The Post on Friday 8th May 1931 was an advert:

Thorington House, Hessett
6½ miles from Bury St Edmunds
Poultry, Poultry appliances, Plant and Farming Stock
Including: 600 Head of pedigree poultry,
The farm implements & House Furniture

Lacey N Gooding
Has been favoured with instructions from Mr F T H Godden,
who is leaving the District, to sell by Auction, on Monday next,
May 11th 1931 Commencing at 12-30 o'clock

It has been said that a chimney fire started and the building was burnt down, but I can find no records as to when this happened. It was never to be rebuilt.

Lane Farm

LANE FARM, formerly called Winters Farm, was a traditional L-shaped, timber framed and thatched 16th Century farmhouse, with surrounding farm buildings, two ponds and about 200 acres of land.

In the 1851 Census George Hubbard was living in Hubbards Lane and was recorded as a farmer. He was probably at Lane Farm which was then known as Hubbards Farm. By the 1861 Census George Hubbard was still farming in Hubbards Lane.

In 1871 William Winter is working as Farm Bailiff at Park Lake, which is further up the lane towards the village of Drinkstone, and there is no mention of George Hubbard or Lane Farm. Looking at the 1881 Census, William Winter is a farmer in Newports Lane, which on the 1855 map is Hubbards Lane.

In 1891 William Winter is a farmer and employer at Old House Lane Farm in Old Lane, which is off Hubbards Lane, to the right.He probably rented the land and farm as the owner was J R Hargreaves who lived in Drinkstone Park.

In the East Anglian Daily Times, Tuesday 21st September 1920 is a notice for:

Sale by Auction
SATURDAY, October 9th, WINTERS FARM, HESSETT.
3 miles from Thurston and 7 from Bury St Edmunds.
5 Horses, 12 Head of Neat Stock, 9 Swine, 120 head of Poultry
Collection of Agricultural Implements, Gears,
Harness etc, by direction of Mr J Jewers, whose tenancy expires.

It had been a tenanted farm belonging to a Mr Hargreaves of Drinkstone Park Estate for many years and then after the Second World War, like many estates, it was split up and sold.

Mr Valentine bought Lane Farm in 1941 or 1942. In about 1947 Mr Valentine invented the "Valentine Sugar Beet Hoe" which when connected to a tractor hoed the rows between the sugar beet to keep them free from weeds. The machine was produced by an engineering firm at Stowmarket.

Early in the 1960s the thatched house was pulled down and another built in its place.

Malting Farm

THE NEW farmhouse at Malting Farm was built in 2010/11 after the demolition of a 1960's grain barn. The neighbouring original farmhouse was renamed Harecroft House, taking the name from the field closest to the property.

The new farmhouse was designed for Graham and Klair Bauly by a local architect using architectural references across the ages, the design being based

Malting Farmhouse.

around a hall house, complete with an oak mullion window. It is a four bed-room property of block construction with a rendered finish and a clay tile roof.

Although thoroughly modern building techniques were used, all tradesmen were locally sourced, using a team from the Bradfield Baptist Chapel. The oak windows were made in Rougham and the kitchen was also manufactured there although by a different tradesman.

The house is heated by a ground source heat pump, the underground pipes for the system are in the adjacent meadow.

Harecroft House

THE PROPERTY now called Harecroft House was originally the farmhouse for Malting Farm until a new Malting Farmhouse was built next door in 2010. When the original Malting Farmhouse was built it was a thatched house. The maltings were on the other side of the road.

In the 1841 Census, William Canham was farming on the Great Green but for more than 50 years the farm was owned by Joseph Tiffen. According to the Census records for that period, the farm was called Green Farm in 1851, 1861 and 1881 but in 1871 and 1901 it is recorded as Malting Farm and in 1891 the name is Old Hall Lane Farm. Mr Tiffen died in 1902, aged 90.

In Kelly's Directory of 1908, Henry John Raker was living at Malting Farm, Great Green, and was a Farmer and Insurance Agent. Mr Raker sold the farm in 1932 to Mr Arthur Bauly, who was born at Shrubbery Farm in 1896.

The farmhouse was burnt down on Wednesday 10th April 1946 when the thatched roof caught fire, but it was rebuilt in 1947 with a tiled roof to replace the thatch.

Malting Farmhouse, above, with a thatched roof and, below, after it was rebuilt in 1947. It was later renamed Harecroft House.

Shrubbery Farm

IT IS NOT known when the house was built but from the Bury and Norwich Post of February 14th 1827, is an advert for the sale of trees:

> *To be sold immediately 10 Oaks, 11 Ashes and 11 Elms*
> *as they stand upon the farm in the occupation of Mrs Bauly,*
> *at Hessett, within 5 miles of Bury. All the trees are very fine,*
> *and most of them are of large dimensions.*
> *Proposals for purchase to be made to Messrs Le Grice and Son, Bury.*
> *N.B. The Tenant will direct somebody to shew the trees February*
> *21st 1827.*

The paper does not mention the Christian name of Mrs Bauly in 1827. On October 2nd 1896 Shrubbery Farm was bought by Mr Raynham for the value of £452.12s.4d. Mr Raynham planted mature limes and chestnuts alternately along the roadside. In 1898 the front of the house was changed, and the façade added is built of Woolpit White bricks, but inside the original walls of lath and plaster can still be seen.

In 1904 James Philip Bauly, who came from Tostock after 1861, was farming Shrubbery Farm. When James Bauly died on 12th July 1928 his wife Sarah took over running the farm. Sarah Bauly died on 17th August 1943. Bertram Mitcham bought the farm on 27th October 1943. Then from the Bury Free Press is another advert:

> *On Friday October 30th 1943 at 11.30am*
> *The Shrubbery Farm, Hessett*
> *The Live and Dead Farming Stock for the Exors of the late Mr J. P.*
> *Bauly, as previously advertised.*
> *7 Horses, 46 Cattle, 8 Pigs, 30 Poultry, Agricultural implements and*
> *Tractor Machinery*
> *Catalogues Price 3d, Lacey N Gooding, Auctioneer, Bury St Edmunds.*

The kitchen at the back of the house was the dairy. There were no windows only wooden slats, and it was used when the farm had a herd of cows. The bronze beech and lime trees were planted between the existing trees at the front and others were planted along the drive by Mrs Frances Mitcham.

The field named Barratts Meadow was opposite Lane Farm and was used for football and cricket matches as the main Green was not even enough to play on and needed to be made flat. It was then moved to the meadow behind Shrubbery Farm.

In the meadow to the left of Shrubbery Farm stood a cottage where two families lived.The front meadow is where the village held the Coronation games in 1953, when the present Queen Elizabeth II was crowned.

Where Shrubbery Close houses are now was the farmyard where all the farm machinery and stacks of harvested crops were kept. In a field at the back of the Green was a hard pad stand where the Sugar Beet was put ready to be taken to the sugar factory.

Shrubbery Farm.

Hicket Heath Farmhouse

From the Bury & Norwich Post – 21st February 1827:
Capital Farming Stock, Furniture etc at The Heath Farm, Hessett
near Woolpit and Bury.
To be sold by auction by George Bidwell on Monday February 26th 1827,
commencing with the Furniture precisely at Eleven.

It is uncertain when the farmhouse was built, but deeds and records held by the family, show that at the beginning of 1932 Mr Arthur Bauly purchased the farm from John Henry Joseph Raker. Shortly after, on 27th January 1932, Mr Bauly rented Hicket Heath to Mr Raker and then on the 6th April 1935 Mr Bauly sold the farm back to Mr Raker. Mr Raker later sold the farm to a Mr Lyon and Mr Bauly re-purchased Heath Farm from Mr Lyon in 1960.

As told by Olive Catchpole on 15th November 1994:

"There was a vine on the outside of the house and there was a yard at the back with a pump for the water. There was a lovely avenue of elm trees as you went down to the yard from the Hickett Heath gate. As you went into the farmyard there was a flint wall.

"You went into the house by a hallway; to the left there was a huge room and then two steps up to a smaller room where they lived in the winter because it was easier to heat.

"In the kitchen there were white bricks on the floor and the biggest black range you ever did see which took up the whole wall. Over the other side was a huge water tank with a pump. On the chimney breast there were lots of bells with springs.

"There were four bedrooms upstairs but they could only use two because sometime before a tree had fallen on to the roof at the back end and it was never repaired, they were only the servant's rooms anyway. You had to walk outside to the loos down the garden. I remember the boys had a laugh and used to scare themselves when they went down there.

"Will Catchpole (Cliff Catchpole's father) married and lived there for a while after his father died. He was convinced the house was haunted because he always locked the doors before he went to bed. They were half doors and you just put a piece of wood across to lock them and when he got up in the morning the doors had opened of their own accord".

Will Catchpole managed the farm for Mr Raker. There were five sons and six daughters. His grandmother died at the age of 49 years. The gate to the farm is all that is left of the house.

The gate to Hicket Heath Farm.

Hill Farmhouse

HILL FARMHOUSE is a Grade II listed building, formerly known as Wood Hall Farm. It is thought to date from the early to mid 18th Century but was altered around 1930. On the 1841 Census, Thomas Lanchester is Bailiff of Wood Farm but by the 1851 Census it is now known as Hill Farm, with Ephram Taylor farming 180 acres and employing six men.

The building is two storey, timber framed and clad in hardboard sheeting which was plastered. The roof has concrete tiles but was formerly pantiled, and could originally have been thatched. It has a central chimney of 18th century red brick and a 19th century gable chimney to the left. There are small pane steel windows from the 1930s. The entrance porch dates from about 1930 and has a pantiled roof and a boarded and battened door. Inside the oak framing is exposed throughout and every storey post has at its head a well formed scrolled joint. The main beams are chamfered (moulded) and there are back-to-back lintelled open fireplaces.

In one room was a cupboard that had a niche – now gone – which was used during the late 17th Century by Catholics to hide items for the altar. On a wall in one of the rooms is a brick with the name Richard Paxwe inscribed (there do not seem to be any more letters) and the date 1749. To the left of the house there used to be pigsties and before that there were tanning sluices.

Freewood Farm

THE FIRST mention of Freewood Farm is in the 1881 Census when it is being farmed by John Squirrell and employing 14 men and one boy to work the 130 acres. It is probably 16th Century and is timber framed with a pantile roof which was probably thatched many years ago.

Several other farms are mentioned in the 1841 to 1871 Census which I am unable to say whether they were former names of Freewood Farm. The names include Grooms, Kaleys, Raynham and Coopers but the Census does not indicate exactly where the farms were located in the village.

Freecroft Farm

FREECROFT FARM house is a brick and flint house, built before 1801, as in 1801 Michael William Le Heup owned the land (Ref:E3/30/13.16). In the 1841 Census the land was being farmed by Samuel Robinson. Also living with him are his wife and three children and there were nine other people, 14 people in all so the building could have been two cottages.

Taken from the Plan of Allotments for 1850, George Biddell had the farmhouse, buildings and yard. In 1851 Ambrose Burrows is living there with his wife and three children. In 1855 William Walpole was the farmer. In 1859 an indenture between William Walpole and Godfrey Frewer (sic) had a gravel pit on the farm (Ref: E3/30/13.16). Stated in the 1861 Census Godfrey Jewer (sic) is the farmer and employing four men.

In the 1881 Census the farm is being worked by William Chapman and his wife who were employing three men. In the 1871 Census there is no mention of Freecroft Farm but there is mention of Valley Farm three times, one can only assume that one of these are Freecroft Farm.

Living in the house in the 1891 Census is George Game, a farm servant with his wife, three children and their grandson. On the 1901 Census a George Osborne was a horseman on the farm and was living in the farmhouse with his wife and son.

Mr Geoffery Collins owned the farm and land, when he passed away in 1921 the farm was left to Mr and Mrs Barton and family.

According to Kelly's Directory in 1925 Mr Henry Cullen was the farmer of Freecroft Farm which he was still farming in 1933. In the Bury Free Press, November 17th 1934, the farm was sold and bought by Mr Cousins of Ixworth which continued to be a farm and was farmed by Mr and Mrs Barton. When the Barton family retired the house was let and the land is still being farmed, but it is now contracted out.

Green Farm and Green Meadow Cottage

GREEN MEADOW is behind Mullion Barn at the end of the village, on the road to Felsham, and is Grade II listed dating from the early 17th Century with an earlier core and consisting of one storey with attics. It was originally of a three-room plan, with a further room added in the 17th Century to the west end. It is timber framed and plastered with a thatched roof and a central early 17th Century chimney of red brick with a saw-tooth shaft.

The house was originally a farmhouse and then became two cottages and is now one thatched cottage. On a door inside the house is carved the name 'Bauly' as the family lived and farmed there. On the 1838 apportionment only Jemima Bauly's name appears, as her husband John died in 1819.

On the 1841 Census it shows Jemima Bauly living there with her son James and the property is called Green Farm. Jemima is 65 and listed as a farmer. She died in 1847. Her son James Bauly was born in 1809 and died 1898.

Green Meadow Cottage.

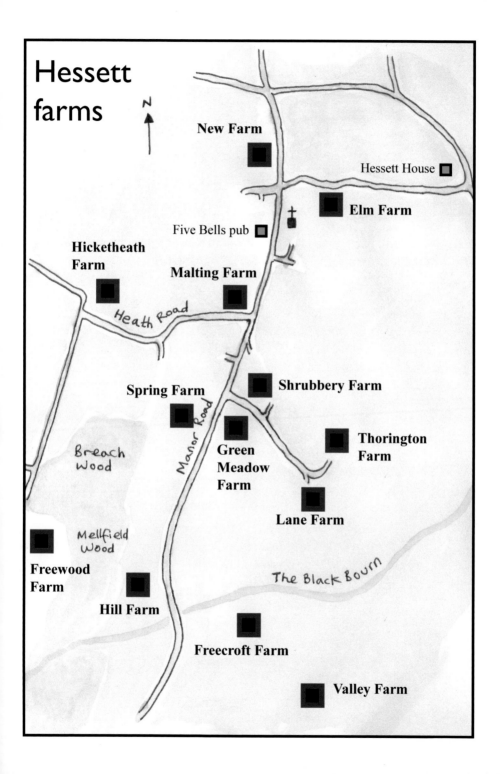

Houses and cottages

Hessett Hall

HESSETT HALL was a manor house and may have resembled some of the surviving timber framed and moated houses in the county, with at least two storeys and many chimneys. In the book "Materials for a History of Hessett" by William Cooke, 1877, (page 81) and from a bequest in the will of Thomas Bacon 1546 (Ref IC500/129/72) it may be inferred that Thomas Bacon had a "Cappella Indotata" in his house which was probably a Catholic private chapel. Considering that Hessett Hall was some distance from the parish church, and close to outlying houses in Bradfield and Rougham, this must have been a great boon to the poor and infirm.

When Lionel Bacon (son of Edmund, 1554-1624) died in 1653 without issue, the manor passed to his eldest sister, Elizabeth, and then to Elizabeth's son Robert Walpole of Houghton in Norfolk who was the father of Sir Robert Walpole, the first Prime Minister. On the 20th December 1699, Sir Robert Walpole (1676-1745) sent a letter from Norfolk to Sir John Mordant at the House of Commons, Westminster saying: "Will travel via Hessett to London".

A 1723 map of Hessett showing Hessett Hall.

In 1708 Aubrey Porter purchased whatever shares were then in the possession of Sir Robert Walpole and appears to have become the owner. Later John Porter inherited The Hall and sold it in 1724 to Thomas Le Heup (Ref E3/22/2.18). Michael Le Heup, Lord of the Manor, purchased the tenement lands abutting Hickett Heath on 19 September 1743.

From Coventry Archives (Ref PA242/2/2) is a document from 24th November 1753: "Michael Le Heup of Hessett (eldest son of Michael Le Heup and wife Elizabeth nee Gery both dec'd) conveys to Thomas Henzell (of Greys Inn, Middlesex, Gent) Hessett manor and land". Then on 27th November 1753 (Ref PA 183/2): "Conveyance to Thomas Henzell, the Manor of Hessett, the Mansion House called Hessett Hall previously occupied by Michael Le Heup deceased, now occupied by Michael Peter Le Heup".

The Hall was destroyed by fire in the 18th Century but no date is recorded and it was never rebuilt. When Michael William Le Heup died in 1809, the manor and advowson passed to his two daughters, Mrs Rogers and Mrs Cocksedge.

In the Bury Post newspaper dated 14th March 1930 (Ref HD526/68/4) it states, on the road leading from Hessett to Rougham and on the right hand side across a meadow is situated the moat which once surrounded it. Square in shape, the internal measurement is from north to south 65 yards, and from east to west 70 yards, the inner sides of the moat are filled with brick work. There is a wooden bridge which spans it at the northwest corner, and just inside the enclosure stand a couple of cottages. The house stood in the enclosure and faced south. Part of the brick edge of the moat surrounding the former hall can be found in a field off Heath Road.

The Mount .... and cleaning out a moat

A MOAT surrounds The Mount at the back of what is now Mount Close. On the 1723 map (Ref E3/22/2.18) this was known as "Old Hall Orchd & Motes" (but with no trace of a building) and could therefore have been the earlier manor site. Although closer to the village it is still a distance from the church. Most halls or main houses were usually nearer to the church. Thedwastre Rural District Council Minutes of 23rd July 1896 record that the Inspector reported that the moat at Hessett required cleaning out (Ref EF500/1/10). It is not clear which moat was referred to as there are three in the village: where Hessett Hall stood, the one at The Mount and at Spring Farm.

The Old Post Office /Anglia Audio Hi Fi Centre

THIS IS A GRADE II listed building dating from the early 16th Century. It is timber framed and plastered. There is a lean-to extension to the right of the shop, dating from the 17th/18th century and 19th Century additions to the rear.

In 1864 Harrod's Directory of Suffolk records that mail came through Bury St Edmunds, which was the post town, the nearest money order office was at Woolpit. The Old Post Office in Hessett opened in 1894 with a shop that sold everything. The first mention of a Post Office in Hessett is in Kelly's Directory of 1896 with William Palmer as sub-post master. The nearest money order office was Beyton and the nearest telegraph office being at Rougham.

The shop and Post Office was run by Mr Bruce until he retired, then it was taken over by William Mills. When he died it passed to his son Charles Mills. In the early 1960s there was a staff of about six people working in the shop and if there was an item you wanted but Charles Mills did not keep it, it would be in the shop either by that afternoon or the next day!

When Mr Mills retired it was bought by Mr Bagg until the Post Office closed in 1976. The shop then moved to the house now called Chapel Cottage, next to Alwyd in The Street, and when it closed there, it went back to the Old Post Office where Mr Bagg's son Eugene took over. He ran the shop as a general store and as Anglia Audio Hi Fi Centre, selling specialist equipment. It finally closed in about 2004 and is now a private house.

The shop and Post Office in about 1920.

Alwyd and Wilwyn

THESE HOUSES, built as one in the late 14th or 15th Century, are Grade II listed. There are alterations from the late 16th Century and mid 20th Century within the building. They are timber framed and plastered with a concrete pantiled roof, which was formerly thatched. The main range comprises an open hall whose cross-entry was probably on the site of the chimney, a storied room is at the left hand end.

The cross wing (Wilwyn) was remodelled in the late 16th Century using base curved wooden timbers. A splayed notch and grooved joint with under-squinted butts at this end of the original structure indicates a possible 14th Century origin.

The unusual names have been given to the properties relatively recently. It is thought that Alwyd means "inglenook fireplace" in Welsh. In the 1940s, Wilwyn was named after the people who lived there, William and Wyn.

In the Daily Mail of February 1st 1995, Hessett was put on the map by two widows, Mrs Bristow and Mrs Payne, who went on a three-year spree across the British Isles with an alleged confidence trickster, a Ms Dodge. Although they had just been friends with the other woman, she had been the trickster and they just enjoyed the travelling. Ms Dodge paid for the hire of Wilwyn for a few weeks and then left the sisters on their own, while she went off with her daughter and never returned.

White Cottage and Fraisnor

THESE TWO houses in Heath Road were built as one farmhouse in the mid/ late 16th Century. It is timber framed and roughcast, with a pantiled roof, sloped at either end. It has a central 16th Century chimney of red brick with a 19th Century chimney to the left.

White Cottage has 20th Century windows and Fraisnor has modern replacement windows. There are 20th Century boarded doors to both houses, the left hand one being at the cross entry position. The inside comprises a cross entry and service room. There are twin service rooms (now united). The chamber above extends over the cross entry, as far as the chimney which backs onto the cross entry. There are unmoulded 16th Century framing exposed and unchamfered floor joists laid flat. The house was extended to the left by one room in the mid 20th Century.

In 1933 the land, which included where Woodcroft is now, and the houses, which were occupied by Mr Bullett and Horace Ottley, were sold. In the photo taken outside Fraisnor the lady in black is Mrs Kate Ottley, the wife of Horace Ottley.

St Anthony

ST ANTHONY was built around 1550, according to deeds held by the owners, and consists of one storey and attics. It is timber framed and plastered with a thatched roof with one 19th Century gables window dormer.

It has a red brick central chimney from the 17th Century and a 19th Century small pane sash window and a mid 20th Century small pane steel window. There is a battened and boarded entrance door and next to it a half-glazed 20th Century door with evidence for clasped purlin roof.

Pipers Cottage

PIPERS COTTAGE is a Grade II listed building dating from the early to mid 16th Century but remodelled in the mid 20th Century. The house

became the laundry for the village in 1921, when Ethel Sturgeon married Charlie Piper and was where the surplices for the church choir were washed, ironed and repaired from before 1914/15 to beyond 1936.

May Cottage

MAY COTTAGE in The Street is a Grade II listed building which probably dates from 1743 as shown on a cartouche on the front wall with the letters IMA above. The cottage is one storey with attics and a two-room lobby entrance plan. Inside the side of the window, near where a door used to be, is a symbol of two circles with a half circle and long line. This may have been to ward off evil sprits from entering the house.

The building was originally two cottages. The left hand side was the original Post Office, run by Mr Bruce. The Post Office then moved to East View, and then to The Old Post Office. Between May Cottage and the wall of The Old Post Office was a bridge which crossed the ditch with a foot-path going to the fields and probably to The Hall, but the path has now gone.

May Cottage today and, above, as two cottages.

Five Bells Cottage

FIVE BELLS Cottage is a Grade II listed building dating from the early 16th Century. It is said that John Bacon the elder named a house on this site as "Reris", and left it to his sister Margaret Fuller.

It is timber framed and plastered and has 19th Century beaded panels with herringbone pargetting. The late 16th Century chimney has large lintelled open fireplaces back-to-back, and one above. One includes the limestone sides of a door frame, probably taken from the Abbey in Bury St Edmunds.

Five Bells Cottage was divided into seven cottages at one time, five cottages where the current is and a further two where the garage now stands.

Five Bells Cottage (right).

Thatched cottages, Heath Road

THERE WERE two rows of thatched cottages with four houses in each row. These were made of clay lump and the clay was probably dug out of the field opposite, where the ponds are now. On the 8th November 1930 (Ref HD526/68/6) one row of houses were burnt down and Shangri-la was built on the site. The fire was caused by a chimney spark from the suriviving row which set the roofs of the other houses alight.

Vipers Hall

VIPERS HALL probably dates from the 17th Century and was originally a timber framed house, but was rebuilt with load bearing walls and rendered externally. The earliest record is in 1814 when the Rev. William Steggall of Thurston purchased the property. It was, many years ago, called Vipers Harp as it stood in a piece of land shaped like a harp.

Vipers Hall was used as a dame school for girls only (as far as is known). Miss French was the teacher and ran the school attended by the Squirrell, Bauly, Mash children and others. Miss French was a single amputee and had more than one wooden leg which had to be changed at intervals during class time.

The Bury and Norwich Post of Friday 8th August 1913 carried the following advertisement for the sale of the property:

Beyton House Estate
Lots 19, 25, 27, and 28, consisting of a useful small holdings, known
as Vipers Harp, Hessett (House, Buildings and 3¼ Acres)
Apply to the Auctioners, 30 Abbeygate, Bury St Edmunds

Hessett House

HESSETT HOUSE was built of brick in 1837. The Rev. Edward Morton Bartlett (born 21st August 1877) was the second son of James Joyce, an engineer of Wimborne, Dorset. Edward Bartlett went to school at Wimborne Grammar School, he then went to Pembroke College, Cambridge and gained a B.A. in 1900. He was ordained Deacon in 1901 and gained an M.A. in 1904.

The Rev. Bartlett had many holdings in churches including Moulsham, Essex -1901–04; Church of St Matthew's, Ipswich - 1904-06; Woolpit, Suffolk – 1906-14; and finally Rector of Hessett, 1914 to 1954.

He lived in a house near the church, which was originally a Rectory. The Rev. Bartlett married Helen Bauly who was living with her family at The Shrubbery, then moved to Hessett House in 1837 when the house was built after her marriage.

Hessett House was extended by adding a flat to the side of the house consisting of a ground and first floor, with the plans being submitted in 1952 (Ref HG500/579(f)). There was an old coach house which stood to the side of the entrance to the house and was pulled down and rebuilt in 1997.

Church Cottage

CHURCH COTTAGE is Grade II listed and the earliest parts of it dates from the late 14th Century. Additions were made to the building around 1500-1530. The building would have looked very different and was originally much smaller. There would have been an open hall with possibly a loft over part of it. The fireplace would have been a central hearth with no chimney and the smoke would have dispersed through the thatch. The roof and eaves level would have been much lower.

In the late 16th Century an upper floor with good chamfered joists were inserted in the hall, and a lintelled open fireplace with limestone piers, which were probably removed from the demolished Abbey of St Edmundsbury. In the 18th Century, a first floor was inserted into the 14th Century hall and that structure was re-roofed. Major alterations in the 1970s included a rear extension and a new higher roof over the entire medieval section. Church Cottage was made into three cottages with a thatched roof. In the 1960s this fell into disrepair and when renovated it was replaced with a tiled roof.

In 2017 the current owners removed 1970s plaster, a gas fire and a modern fireplace to reveal a small inglenook fireplace (date unknown). Further plaster was removed to the left of the inglenook to reveal an almost intact bread oven, complete with what is thought to be a layer of brick insulation over the top. The bread oven was built using bricks manufactured by C. Stutter of Woolpit, Suffolk as a brick has been found stamped accordingly. Entrance to the bread oven is believed to have been through a lean-to at the back of the house.

Church Cottage before restoration in the 1970s.

Church Cottage today and, below, the bread oven to the left of the chimney breast which was discovered during recent renovation work.

Within the house there are signs of superstitious markings over the main fireplace on the bressumer beam, as well as in places where other fireplaces may have been within the house centuries ago. These markings include taper marks over the main inglenook fireplace in the lounge, believed by superstitious occupants to stop the house burning down, and witch marks, carved to ward off evil spirits entering the house.

On the first floor there is also evidence of grooves where window shutters would have originally been pulled across windows at night or to keep the house warm.

The Black House, The Alley

THE ALLEY, Hessett, just behind the school where Bridge Cottage and Peddars Cottage are now, was a track with houses. There was a block of two cottages, a group of four cottages and then The Black House. The Black House was built of clay lump and tarred, and there were two old yew trees on the top of the bank and ditch alongside the alley.

Olive Catchpole lived there when she and her family came to live in Hessett in 1919. She was 10 years old and the family used to get water from the school well. In the kitchen they had a brick oven to the left with a corner cupboard above for cooking utensils and then a little recess. There was another room at the back. The stairs led straight up on to the floor of the first bedroom and then through the door to her parents' room.

At number 4 of the row of four cottages lived Mr Sturgeon who was a wheelwright. His cottage was pulled down to make way for a garage for one of the houses.

Peddars Cottage.

Mullion Barn

MULLION BARN is a Grade II listed building and is 20 metres north-west of Green Farmhouse. It probably dates from the early 17th Century. It was said to have five alcoves, timber framed and weather-boarded. It had a corrugated iron roof, which was once thatched. There was a lean-to roofed porch at the centre of the west side with boarded barn doors. A lower attached range contained a trough and a stable at the south end had a 20th Century roof but may have been of 16th/17th Century origin.

The barn, which had almost collapsed, was bought in 2007 and has been renovated and converted into a house and holiday cottage.

Below, Mullion Barn with an iron roof and, left, after it had been stripped back to the timber frame and renovated.

Spring Cottage and the Council Houses in Manor Road

Mrs Olive Catchpole remembers Spring Cottage and the new Council Houses in Manor Road:

SPRING COTTAGE was a little thatched cottage where the council houses numbers 9 and 10 stand now in Felsham Road (Manor Road). The date on the wall was 1692 and it was last owned by Mr Fred Squirrell.

Claud and Dolly Borley lived in one end and Cliff and I [Olive Catchpole] and the two boys lived in the other. We had to get water from the pump in the kitchen of the Green Meadow Farmhouse across the road.

The bedroom of our sons, Paul and Bill, was over the living room of Claud's so they could hear everything that Claud and Dolly said. They used to have a programme on the wireless called "Bright and Early" followed by "Thought of the Day". The boys heard the announcer say "and that is the end of Bright and Early for today" and Claud was heard to say "bloody good job too".

In Claud's garden at Spring Cottage there were some beautiful fruit trees, including a Prince Albert cooking apple and a Beauty of Bath, one of the first eating apples to be ripe for picking.

NUMBER 9 and 10 Felsham (Manor) Road were the first two council houses to be built and every Sunday afternoon the people in the village used to walk up to look to see how far the building had got.

There was great speculation as to who was going to be the first to live in them. We were lucky, along with Claud and Dolly Borley – so we just moved across the garden and then they pulled the old house down. Then the council built two more houses. There should have been six but they messed Mr Fred Squirrell about so much he would only let them build four!

At first we still had to go across the road to Green Farm for our water, but when we eventually had running water it was so cold and clear.

Memories: Hessett and rural life

THE FOLLOWING chapter is of people's memories which have been collected and written down on paper exactly as they were recorded between 1994 and 2011. It is a nice way of seeing how people were brought up, how they made their own amusements and what happened in village life. Although some of the memories are not of village life they may still be of interest.

Mrs Kathleen Bauly
Malting Farm, Hessett, 26th June 1994

In 1939 the Americans were stationed at Rougham. I used to help look after 12 of them when they were away from home. They were the USAF weather men. On their time off they used to cycle over to mine, picking blackberries on the way. I used to make them blackberry and apple pie to take back to the camp at Rougham.

They were only young men, there were several 21st birthdays while they were here. I first saw them when they came asking whether we had any eggs and I did not want to see them at first. I said to my husband, Arthur, that I did not want anything to do with them in the yard because they had a bad reputation – they used to get the young girls of 13 or 14 drunk in the pub and then they used to be sick all over the green. Anyway, Arthur said to me that our boy Martin might be away from home some day so we had better make them feel welcome. They turned out to be nice boys and we had some happy times. Martin was about seven years old at the time. Their Captain was so grateful for the hospitality we gave to his men that when he left he presented us with the cheese container on the sideboard. He had wrapped it up in his vest when he brought it over.

Some of the boys had a bad time because they had lost some of their mates. They used to be very emotional and upset. One of the older men was in such a state. He was a dentist back in America and his wife was having a baby. As soon as he heard that he had a little girl he was OK. There was another one who stood apart from the rest, it turned out that when he had gone back I found out that he was a millionaire – in the shoe manufacturing business. Yes, they said that Greg was a millionaire. The boys came on and off for three years. They used to help me milk the old house cow, churn the milk and make it into butter. They had never seen anything like that before. My grandson, Graham, still wears the flying jacket of one the men.

There were thousands of men at Rougham. The planes used to go out over Malting Farm. My niece, Brenda, came from London for a rest once because they had a bad time in London. The funny thing was, the first morning she was here, she came screaming downstairs, "Aunt, there's one coming!". "Who's coming?" I said. It was down in a minute and it went down with a bang over in the woods behind Spring Farm. It was a doodlebug [V-1 flying bomb]. They came over towards the end of the war, they used to set the oil lamps dancing. In the farmhouse I had no electricity, I used to cook over oil. I had a Triplex cooker, I used to cook two ducks in one oven and two ducks in the other. Do you know, I had so many letters from the airmen's mothers grateful for what I had done for them – for their boys. They wanted to know how to make Yorkshire Pudding.

During the war Arthur was a warden in the Home Guard. He used to parade up and down in the village looking for lights that were on and making sure that

A story from the Bury Free Press about the 1946 fire which destroyed Malting Farmhouse.

Picturesque Farmhouse Burnt Down

curtains were pulled. We first heard of the war on the radio and as time went on we started to have convoys driving through the village with a build up of planes at Rougham.

In April 1946 Malting Farmhouse was destroyed by fire. It was the electricity that caused the fire, you know. We hadn't even received the bill for the wiring job when the fire broke out. I remember it so well. Martin was home from boarding school, and I thought I heard him on the landing but it was all the trip switches going off. You see they had attached them to the chimney. Then of course the whole place went up. The roof had gone in an hour. At first they thought that it was a chimney fire but it was the wiring. Arthur had gone to market at Bury that Wednesday so they had to go and find him. Sir Keith Agnew was a young man then – he came to help – he was the first there. He pulled out all the furniture, he did so well. He got a hose and tried to put the fire out but he couldn't do anything.

Arthur, my husband, was born at the Shrubbery [Shrubbery Farm]. He was one of nine children born there. Jim his older brother was just 12 months old when they moved to Hessett. I was Kathleen Bull and my family came from Brick House Farm, Hitcham, and we married in 1934 on 15th April. When Arthur was in hospital for a year I had to manage the farm, and the old house cow wouldn't let anyone go near it. So Phil Lawson from Ixworth had to take it off our hands. Arthur lived in Elm Farm first in 1921 and just as he came out of the Army his father put him in there. He was in the First World War in the trenches for four years. He was in the horse artillery. His horse was shot from under him.

Arthur wanted us to go on the telephone after I had given birth to Martin. He had to go up to Mr Mills at the shop and phone five times to talk to the doctor. He got fed up with that so said he'd go on the phone after that. I had a very long labour and Martin was born at home. They used all the instruments and I was in bed for a month after that, I had a rough time. There was a midwife and Dr. O'Mara. Just as the nurse had sorted me out and the doctor was about to leave I had a haemorrhage and so the doctor had to come rushing back in again, I had a very rough time.

A man set light to our straw stacks deliberately one morning. Three or four of the stacks were well alight when the fire engines got here with the Police. We thought that it was an aeroplane that had caused it as one had gone over just before the fire was discovered. The police tried to make our young farm boy own up – they really tried to force him into saying that he did it. But it turned out to be the man who sees to the engine on the threshing tackle. At the time he was up at Freecroft Farm and he had said to his mates, "I set them alight this morning when I came to work. They are well alight by now". Well, he went to court and then to prison but he's gone a bit mad. His excuse was that there were far too many stacks to thresh and that they'd never get through them all. The stack yard was up where Mount View house is now in Heath Road.

Miss Kathleen Mash
8th August 1994

Vipers Hall, Hessett was a small 'dame school' [dame schools were small private schools run by women]. The teacher was Miss French whose father was an artist. Miss French had a wooden leg and she used to send the children to fetch her leg. Miss Jones was the other teacher, who was the parson's daughter. The parson was Rev. Jones, he was almost blind. At the school was Dolly (Dorothy Squirrell), Dorothy Bayer's grandmother.

We always went across for tea at Shrubbery Farm to Mrs Sarah Bauly. She used to make the most delicious rusks (traditional Suffolk recipe). Mr James Bauly always used to sit at the head of a very large table and I can only remember him cutting slices and slices of home made bread to spread with butter. We always used to play with the Bauly children. We walked everywhere mostly but on Sunday we were allowed to cycle, we had fixed wheel bikes. My sister Betty was the adventurous one – she use to fly down Beyton hill with her feet on the handlebars.

Miss French provided the children with a lunch. I always remember mashed potatoes which were cooked with eggs. Gwen, my sister, would not touch the spinach because there was fried egg on the fork, and she has never liked spinach to this day. We used to walk along the road which was just a cart track. We used to get our milk from Shrubbery Farm, we fetched the milk in the can – we had skimmed milk in one can and full cream milk in the other.

We passed the Five Bells Cottages, we always saw a jackdaw that someone had as a pet. Mr Bussey lived there – he often did odd jobs for my father. Father would pay him and say to him, "Make sure you get home with that and don't spend it on the way". Mr Bussey always had a hole in his hat. In his cart he had a ticking clock. They were a lovely looking family; Mrs Bussey always had such rosy cheeks.

I remember that the woods at the back of Spring Farm used to be full of wild strawberries and we used to meet up with the Bauly children and pick pounds of them. Then mother would make jam – it was delicious. We picked mushrooms from the fields, we never had to ask for permission.

Captain and Mrs Hughes
Hill Farm, Hessett, 11th August 1994

Mrs Hughes: The little school was at The Poplars, in Beyton, at first and it moved to The Shrubbery in 1948. Peter, our son, went when he was about six. Then it moved to East View, on the Green with Ruth Mills. The Thurlow boys also went there. Once, when Ann Mitcham had measles and was in quarantine, the school went over to a room at Mrs Daniels house for three weeks. I remember that Mrs Mitcham was furious but we told her that the children's education had to go on. Peter Mills then got meningitis.

Captain Hughes: When I took over the Parish Council I ruled it with a rod of iron. I was co-opted on, I wasn't elected. After the war I managed to get us some council houses in Hessett. They were all going to Felsham, because the chairman of the district council lived there. So I went to see him to see why we didn't get these council houses. Anyway, we eventually got some. I also helped to get a bridge across the ford in Hessett Street in the 1950s. Everyone was getting stuck in their motor cars in the water when we had had some heavy rain.

Helen Bauly, who was the daughter of Mr and Mrs Bauly of Shrubbery Farm, was Edna and Lily Barber's godmother; Helen lived at home. We would hire Monks Wood for the shooting season (this would be Major Nicholson and my father). Helen used to let us use the front room at the Shrubbery to have a meal, we would take a hot pot in a hay box.

Jim Bullett, who lived on The Green, worked for Mrs Hughes at Hill Farm. At one time we had 100 pigs and thousands of chickens. I owned a Standard Fordson Tractor and it didn't have any tractor wheels but Mann Egerton's found some old bus wheels which fitted perfectly. When people used to get stuck in the Manor Wash they used to come to ask us to help pull them out. I used to ask them where they had come from because if they had come a distance the engine would be dry and warm enough to get started again. We would offer them tea and then would pull them out and the engine would cough and splutter up the hill.

When we arrived here in 1946 old William Mills was still delivering groceries in a pony and cart. Peter, our son, went to help him and one day he tipped him 2d. Old Bert (who married Sarah Bullett) was head gardener at Hessett House and he looked after us when we first arrived in Hessett. He advised us to keep some pigs and hens and then we would always know where the house keeping money was coming from. He would never accept more than 1/9d (8½p) per hour because he could work that out himself. He had a daughter, Mabel, who lived at Risby who was a parlour maid to Sir Malcolm Sergeant. I took him one day to see her and when he got home he stepped out of the car and said, "There, we have done well, we have got there and back in one day". It was his first trip in a car. When he was courting Sarah he was known as 'cook's young man'. Old Mrs Squirrell lodged with him and another lady at the lodge (the house at the end of The Green) and he always took his ladies a cup of tea in bed on a Sunday morning.

Mrs Hughes (who was a Miss Lay before she married Captain Hughes and she lived in Rougham House between 1926 – 1943): When Stephen Agnew was 17 he ran the Home Guard. Old Collins the gardener said that he was a good chap and looked after us. Rougham Hall was bombed during the war when old Sir George was there. He never went back after that, he didn't know why or what had happened. They reckoned there must have been some lights on at Rougham Place where the troops were or the planes were just off loading their bombs on the way home. Mr Barber, the gamekeeper for Mr Hargreaves, had quite a reputation. He would shoot anything that moved - cats, dogs, anything.

Edna Hazelwood (nee Barber): Helen Bauly did not want anyone to know that she was engaged to Rev. Bartlett so she wore the ring round her neck, but everyone knew. She used to take us Barber children to Sunday School.

Martin Bauly
Elm Farm, Hessett, 5th August 1994

Martin's father was Arthur Bauly of Malting Farm, Hessett. Arthur Bauly's horses were Proctor (a Suffolk), Prince (Percheron), Smiler (Suffolk), Glory (Clydesdale), Captain (black horse) and Doddy (a Shire).

The last horses to go were in 1955. The first tractor Arthur had was a standard Fordson, the clutch and the footbrake were all in one. One day I had a cultivator on the back and I was turning round trying to get the cultivator to lift and then I found the front wheels of the tractor over the pond. The next tractor we had was a David Brown Super Crop Master.

In October 1924 the workmen on the farm were Tom Cocksedge (Old House Lane Cottage), E. Otley, F. Green, C. Frost, Frank Harris (father of Arthur Harris), and E. Cousins. In 1946 Gerald Mills was paid £4 per week for 48 hours, starting at 6.45am, with breakfast at 8.30am.

In April 1946 when we had the fire [at Malting Farm], the men working for us were Herb. Bullett (Jim Bullett's father), Old Cocksedge, Fred Piper (cousin to Harold Piper), Denis Cocksedge and Alf Easter, an evacuee living in Vipers Hall. Wages then were £1.12s.0d per week. They all came down off the fields to get the furniture out of the house. The firemen had to get water out of the pond. After a while they all concentrated on dampening down the thatch on the barn alongside. I can remember picking up a pail we had outside the back door, we used it for potato peelings. I tipped them out and ran to the pond to fill it with water but it was useless, I'll never forget that as long as I live.

The women used to wait till after the field had been cut and then go gleaning. They wore a big apron and collected the ears of the corn around the edge of the field to take home to feed the chickens or geese for Christmas. Ray Harris kept pigs down near Barbers Field. He now lives in a bungalow near Drinkstone Windmill.

I can remember when I was about 15 years old I wanted to go to Bradfield Combust to collect this machine called a swath turner with one of the horses. I begged my parents to let me go. I set off with a horse called Duke. Well, the horse got as far as the Manor Wash (between Hessett and Felsham) and refused to go through the water. As hard as I tried I could not make it go through – so of course I had to get off and lead it through. I had an awful job to get this machine home because it had three wheels and went all over the road. Coming home the old horse just walked through the water as good as gold. It had taken all day; it was a cold January day and had been snowing and when I got home it was dark. Another time we got stuck in the Wash with the car, so father had to walk up to the Bartons at Freecroft Farm to get help. They came with a horse and pulled us out.

On the farm sales particulars they used to make reference to the nearest station because very few people had cars. They even had facilities to put the animals on the train in special wagons. There were cattle pens at Thurston Station. There was once a pub up Heath Road (last house before the thatched row). There was also a bowling alley up there in a long shed.

Jewers from Rattlesden farmed at Winters Farm (Lane Farm). He used to tie his horse and cart to the gates of Hessett House and creep up on his men to see if they were working. One day when he had too much to drink the men un-hitched the horse and put the shafts of the cart through the gate posts and then hitched the horse on again on the other side of the gate so when Jewers tried to get in to drive home he couldn't understand why it wouldn't go very far.

Harry Cocksedge used to stand on his head with his head in a bucket and sing a song. That was his party piece when there wasn't much else to do. I was about 16 when I used to go rabbiting with him and his son Oliver. Claud Borley was the roadman, he used to start little trees off in his garden when they were just conkers. Two of the trees are growing in the garden of Elm Farm today (1994). He always reckoned he used to work so hard that he would have to cool his scythe off in the pond. One day I had a bad back. Annabelle, my sister, kept her pony in the meadow opposite Elm Farm. I jumped on it and fell right over the other side and when I stood up my backache had gone. Mr W Valentine used to take me to a lot of the exhibitions.

Before 1943, my father had some cattle down on the Park and one day this cow was ill so father went to get the vet, and left me with the cow. He was gone for a long time and it began to get dark and I was really frightened. I was about 10 years old at the time. The owls began to hoot and the moon came up and it was really spooky near the woods. They came eventually but the cow died. Mr Turner was the vet from Bury, he was always in a hurry and couldn't stop long. "Must be getting on my way Mr Bauly," he'd say. But he would always stop a bit longer if Dad offered him a whisky.

Mum kept hens at the back of the farm, I threw some eggs on the roof one day and mum saw all the yolks running down. In 1955 the Milk Marketing Board tested the water from the farm well and decided it wasn't clean enough to clean the dairy floor even though we had used water from the well for years. I even had the cows already in calf. We did not have the piped water then so we had to sell the cows.

W N Valentine (William Norman), 1917-98
Old Bucks Farm, Drinkstone (also known as Chantry Farm), 5th August 1994

I was asked to join this kind of secret service way back in 1937 when I was at Old Bucks Farm. We were sabotage secret undercover agents and we used the Home Guard as a cover after the war started. The powers that be thought even in 1937 that the Germans would invade via Harwich and travel up to Manchester. I was taught how to use explosives and how to prime bombs and my headquarters was in Sicklesmere; our targets were to be railway lines, telegraph poles used for communications and their vehicles.

We were taught how to put these magnetic bombs onto the petrol tanks of the invading army. We were on our own – we were to act as individuals. Do the job and disappear into the countryside again. I had to go for training at Stoke Holy Cross near Norwich. It was there that I saw my first radar scanner and then knew that this is how we would know that the Germans were coming. I was in this all through the war but gradually as the aerodromes were built at five mile intervals, more military were here, so my job sort of diminished as they took over the responsibility. I drove a Morris car and used to collect a man from Lavenham and another from Sicklesmere and go up to Norwich for training. That's how I knew how to use explosives to blow up the tree trunks later.

Second World War: During the war the "Coloured Americans" were at Drink-stone Park and it was their job to move the bombs around when they were needed from Thetford. [The US Army segregated their troops when they were stationed in Britain during the war.] They would travel in a convoy of about 12 to 24 lorries, the back one pushed the front one nose to tail as fast as the road could take them, they were a mad lot.

Every night in the summer the street was full of people going to get water from the well which was opposite the pub, which is still in Five Bells Cottage. The dyke off Lime Tree Close was a very deep ditch which led across to the allotments, but people used to throw their rubbish in there and there used to be numerous complaints. Not so much paper as there was not the packaging as there is today – it was mostly old bikes or garden rubbish.

Education: There was an overall education policy although the people in the village would not be aware of it. There was a different policy for the cities like Manchester, Glasgow and Cambridge, these were the centres of learning and of higher education. The lesser village schools in the country came under an agricultural policy and the children were to have a more vocational education in order to be farm labourers, craftsmen, carpenters etc. They were not to be given the opportunity to go on to higher education, so even though Mother (Edna Valentine) wrote complaining of the standard of education at Hessett School the national policy was not to provide an academic education for these children.

Barbers Field: At the bottom of the lane called Hubbards Lane there is a field known as Barbers Field, since a family called Barber had lived in the Game Keepers Cottage. Edna's father was the gamekeeper for John Hargreaves of Drinkstone Estate. On this field there was a thin strip of land that he used to rear pheasants, with an old caravan in which he used to keep all his bits and pieces of equipment. It was a bad do, he lost half or all of his pheasants one year; whether it was a fox or bad weather I can't remember but he was very upset. Mr Barber's daughter Lily was just a baby; this all happened in 1931/34. The lane down to the Keepers Cottage was always under water all winter and in a very bad state; I should think that he would earn as a game-keeper about 25 shillings a week in a rent free house.

Mr Bullett lived in a cottage (plot 114 on the 1884 map) and he used to come up to the house to get water every day out of the well. Mr Mitcham built a bungalow for Mr Bullett. The local authority paid him £60 per year for 40 years, it was built in 1949/50 and in 1950 another two plots were sold. The cottage (plot 91 on the 1884 map) is where Gordon Harris lived. When Mr Mills built a house on the corner of the green there was a bit of a hoo-ha about the access off the green. In 1950/51 the council houses were built near Spring Farm.

The cottage (plot 128 on the 1884 map) is where Mr Harbutt lived. The Bauly family used to graze livestock on the village green. The bakers at Rougham were brothers (one was called Jack), they delivered bread for 4d a loaf.

The road or track through the village was like a piece of road suitable for a cart to pass over; there was a part for the cart wheel, then a piece of grass and then another place for the other cart wheel. Around 1934 the road was made up with tar with stones thrown on top, and rolled down with a heavy roller. It was quite an occasion and all the children came out to watch.

In 1933 each electric pylon cost £19 and in 1946 the cable came from Rougham. It cost £72 to bring it to Lane Farm. Mr Mitcham and Mr Bauly and myself shared the £72 between us making it £24 each. It cost £25 to wire the house at Lane Farm by the electricity company; it was all taken over ground by poles. I remember the day the electricity was switched on for the first time – it was in the afternoon and we could not believe how dirty the house was. Of course up to now we had only used paraffin lamps. We had a TV in 1947.

On the farm the cows brought in a monthly cheque. At first we milked by hand and the Ministry of Agriculture, Fisheries and Food said that it was not clean enough so we put in a parlour and then milked by machine. We had 10 Ayrshire cows from Scotland, father went up by train to buy them. Then we moved from Ayrshires to Friesians, we used to get about seven churns a day – 80 gallons of milk. We had 24 cows maximum but one day we lost five cows from bloat.

In 1953 we kept broiler hens in a shed 150 x 40 feet, they caught fowl pest and we dug a hole and buried them all. In 1959 we rebuilt the house.

I did the combining for Mr Bauly – and got my money back that way and even made a profit. At first we used to cut it with the binder and cart it to the stack, then the threshing drum would come. They were grumpy old men, if the stack wasn't in the right place they would blame everyone except themselves. We had to palm their hands to keep them in a good temper. In 1950 Dorothy and George Wright moved from Kiln Farm, Woolpit to Elm Farm, Hessett.

On 13th June 1945 there was an outing of farmers to the Ford Works at Dagenham. Miss Rouse from Beyton took mother and Elizabeth was born. Mother (Eliza Valentine) delivered eggs to Thurston Station by horse and cart, which were sent to Manchester every 10 days - five or six wooden cases, 360 eggs in one case.

Andersons of Woolpit delivered the meat and Liptons delivered the groceries. I went to school at Bradfield St George, it was three to four miles away and I walked for the first two years, I was five years old then and was ill. After that I went to Felsham School, then I went to Lord Wandsworth College, Hampshire. A Mr Bay Kinsey – a Felsham family, well he had a sister who was married to a land agent in Farnham, Surrey. J Arthur Egar came to see mother about the College. I can't remember but Egar had sold the estate and the Lord Wandsworth Trustees had bought it. Lord Wandsworth was M.P. for the Stowmarket Division and he wanted children from Suffolk with one parent to get preference. I travelled from Felsham to Bury Bus Station and then by train to Liverpool Street. I was about 12 years old, we wore a badge and someone met us off the train. From there we went by train from Waterloo to Winchfield. I was there from 1929 to Christmas 1934 and then I went back to the farm.

In 1932 I attended the Boy Scouts International Jamboree in Hungary. We were away for three weeks, it costs us £15 and we had to earn that money before we could go. We went by train from Winchfield to London, Dover, Ostend and then across Europe to Budapest. I remember the train had wooden seats; we were all very apprehensive and excited The Germans brought out the brass bands and gave us a royal welcome in Cologne. There were only six of us boys plus a master at the school called Brown. It took two days to get there and there were 2000 boys from all over Britain.

Lane Farm: In 1949 we grew tulips on the 10 acre field. A Dutchman named Hemskirk would supply the bulbs under contract, we would grow them, he would sell them and we would share the profit. We took a sample to the Geest Company and they said they would buy them for £6000. We had to plant them by hand. Arthur Harris, Harold Piper (Muriel's brother), Mr Gant, Mr Turner, and Mr Wilding bagged the tulips after the heads had been taken off. The flowers were sent to Spitalfields Market in London, Geest supplied the cartons. We did not grow any more because the Dutchman disappeared the next season. Lily Sturgeon also worked piece work there.

Sugar Beet: In 1934 the Sugar Beet Factory opened in Bury St Edmunds. The bank would lend you money on the full growth of the sugar beet once it was established at 4% interest. The men used to chop out the sugar beet and were paid 9d to 1 shilling per chain, which was 22 yards, both would check the amount of work done with the chain.

In 1963 a man – Vic Baker – drove into the yard and said that they needed more gravel to extend the runway at Shepherds Grove. Then in 1964 the St Ives and Gravel firm was extending the runway at the aerodrome and I had noticed that there was a lot of flint on the field when I ploughed; we bulldozed a hole 20ft deep. The Air Ministry supplied all the equipment and the lorries and paid 10/- per load.

William Valentine, right, on the back of his invention - the Valentine sugar beet hoe - in 1949.

Harry Stimpson
Stowlangtoft Nursing Home, 18th November 1994

Mr and Mrs Maskey lived at the top of Hubbards Lane (Old Lane), to the left hand side of the fork; the cottage got burnt down. I remember the Maskeys' fire well, it started in the middle of the night. The dogs had started to bark and they woke us up. The roof was well alight by then, it was a chimney fire. I think, although I am not sure, that it was called Thorington House.

Mr Godden the Scout Master lived in an old tin hut further round the corner, he made it into a house and lived there. They all got water from the Old Farm well. I remember the old well; one morning as we were having breakfast, there was such a lumber. The top had fallen in and the whole of the wooden top had collapsed.

I can remember the first night we arrived at the Old Lane Farm. We had come from Soham and brought 200 Light Sussex chickens just at the point of lay – we had put them in the sandpit just in the side meadow. Anyway, a fox killed the lot. We didn't have foxes in Soham so we had not given it a thought. We had three or four house cows. Mother used to make the butter and also the bread in the oven. We used to take the eggs to the market and get 1/- per dozen for them. We would always get a flush of eggs in March, and then you'd pickle them in the winter in water glass. We would put them in a five gallon earthenware jug and they were not cooked beforehand. They would keep as long as you wanted that way.

I lived in Old Lane Farm for 11 years with my father and family from 1921 as a tenant of Mr Hargreaves. Father stayed a few more years after I left. We came from Soham and kept mainly pigs, cows and horses.

The Manor Wash down the Felsham Road (Manor Road) was just a ford and the water used to get quite deep in the winter after the heavy rains. So much so that when we went across in the pony and trap we had to hold our feet up out of the water as it used to come up as far as the floor of the trap. The pony and trap used to hold two people and a third person if the back tail was put down. We would go off to Bury Market on a Wednesday in the pony and trap and for the seven miles it used to take about 45 minutes. We would leave the pony and trap at Pettits Stables at the top end of Woolhall Street while we were at the market. The policeman in Beyton used to say: "I'll be in Quaker Lane when you come back – you make sure you've got your lights on". You see we used to try to come through there without our lights on to try to save the candles in the carriage lamps. As the candle burnt you would push it up and there was one on each side of the trap. The police always tried to catch us as we came through. When it was cold you would have a blanket over your legs.

While you were at the market you would go to the Corn Exchange with your sample of corn to see if you could get a good price for it from the merchants. You would also buy your seed for the next year. When you had agreed a price you would bag up the corn and the merchant would come the next week with his wagon and two horses and cart it away. He would perhaps sell it on to another merchant. There were 16 stone bags of barley, 12 stone bags of oats, 18 stone bags of wheat and 19 stone bags of beans. At first we used to cut the corn with three horses and a binder, one man on the back and another who would stand up the sheaves to keep them dry. You would then cart it to the yard and put it into a stack.

Downing of Norton used to come and thresh it. To keep the steam engine going we had a water cart that we filled up at the pond and then we would pull it over to the stack alongside the engine. Of course 80 years ago men cut it with scythes and their wives would follow tying it up.

Old Mr "Duttle" Bullett lived in the double thatched cottages in the Old Lane and he worked on the land for the Stimpsons. I remember one Sunday the boys in the village, about six or eight of the lads, got a lorry party together and they went to Felixstowe for the day. Anyway, when Duttle came to work the next day father said to him, "How are you Duttle, what did you see then?" "There was a master big pond there Guv, you couldn't see the other side". Of course he meant the sea – most of the men had never been out of the village let alone to the seaside.

We had five horses on the farm; Smart and Blossom, I can't remember the other names. The horses were shod at the blacksmith on the village green at Beyton – a Mr Clark. It cost about 10/- for a set of shoes. If we were taking load of pigs to the market on a frosty morning we would have Mr Clark put some rough nails onto the horses' shoes so they did not slip on the ice. A man's wage was about £1 per week in those days.

I was a special constable during the war and I did my duties at night because I was working during the day. Our main duties were to make sure that there were no lights showing. I was a special constable for 10 or 12 years.

We used to play tennis in the field at the end of the garden at Old Lane Farm. Then we played at Beyton Rectory on the tennis court there. We did have a Hessett Lawn Tennis Club. In the winter we had a dance once a week in the Rector's house. The young ones had a Christmas panto and then perhaps we would get a bus load up to go to the theatre.

Ron Hazelwood
8 Quaker Lane, Beyton.

Ron Hazelwood married Edna Barber who was the post lady for Beyton and Hessett for many years

I used to go round and see Edna and the 'horrors' used to say, "Go on, give her a kiss", cheeky monkeys! 'Horrors' was the nickname given to the evacuees at Ixworth Abbey. During the war all our letters were censored. We wrote letters and gave them to the officer in charge, he would read it and cut things and cross things out and then photo it, reduce its size to about 4-inches square called an airgraph. The postman would then deliver that to Edna.

For Edna, months went by and she did not hear from me and then she would get several at once. Edna sent me food parcels, cakes, apples and cigarettes. Well, it took eight months to reach me. The cake was mouldy and we kicked it round like a football, the apples had gone like prunes and the juice had gone all over the cigarettes. When I came out of the army in June 1946 we took a job at Chippenham Hall for one year.

I was Corporal Ron Hazelwood, Royal Signal Corp at the 1st Suffolk Regiment at Bury, Queens Regiment, then Norfolks, then USA army for six months. You just got transferred, then finally in the Norfolk Regiment I was a fighting soldier. Three years in the desert in North Africa, Battle of el-Alamein, Tunis then Italy. I sailed from Greenock on the Blue Ribbon Line (same as Queen Mary). The ship was a passenger ship for 300 but we had 4,000 troopers aboard. We didn't see land for 56 days, I was dreadfully sick.

Edna Hazelwood delivering post to Jimmy Bauly at Spring Farm.

During the war I was more worried about how I would get home – it had been so awful going out there. I came back by land through Switzerland and France. The ship was called Louis Pasteur. I was three years in the desert, two years in Italy and one year in Greece. El-Alamein started in October at 10pm, went on all night, 700 guns firing at each other, sandstorm and dust. When we were given orders we just drove into the desert, over bodies, we could not see where we were going. Mr Churchill came to see us one day. The King came as well, to Tripoli in North Africa. He came to see us and to knight one of the corporals. I was given the job of driving the water cart. The taps had to be full on to lay the dust before he came.

Churchill used to come up to us and say, "All you've got to say when the war is over is that you've been in the 8th Army and you'll get a job anywhere". Of course, we knew this wasn't right. We used to eat barley bread – just like dog biscuits. I caught malaria – I've had it once since I've been home. I've seen men die from it, they were in a terrible state – sweating and hysterical.

Life on the ship, going out, was terrible – ankle deep in sick. The ship wasn't cleaned for three weeks because everyone was ill. Then it was swilled down, you can just imagine the smell – turned your stomachs, lots of men wanted to jump, many went off their heads. Imagine, we didn't know where we were going, no one could tell us anything. We just laid in the passageways because we were all so ill. I just kept wondering how I was going to get back. I was only 19 years old, I met a chap from Stowmarket on the same ship. There was one woman aboard, she was a nurse. Once she stepped over us lying in the passage, I looked up and said to my mate, "That's a woman". He said, "Don't talk rubbish".

There was a time when I could have packed it all in. We had anchored off Aden and they wouldn't let us off, we were desperate. It was a moonlit night and I considered jumping overboard, but the sea was full of sharks, I could see them all swimming around the ship. There were lots of fights, men got bad tempered, but the trouble was soon sorted. One man did have a heart attack and died. We had to line up on the deck and on the deck above he had been strapped to a door they had taken off the ship. They wrapped him up in old clothes and tipped it and it went whoosh into the sea. I'll never forget it.

Our ship was in a convoy of 32. There were enemy submarines all around us. We didn't take a straight course, we zigzagged. We weren't allowed to smoke and there were no lights, we had to creep around. Then the radar would go "ding, ding, ding" and we knew there was a sub underneath, then it all went quiet again. Some ships got hit. Once we had a breakdown and they left a destroyer to guard us while it was repaired. A couple of our men were reading the paper when they fell overboard and the destroyer picked them up. They stayed on the destroyer then for the rest of the time and when they did come off they were "green". The destroyer had twisted and turned and zigzagged doing twice as much as we did. I remember one afternoon there was what was like a shower of stones being thrown over the ship. It was flying fish, just like a flock of swallows.

We had some bullies in the Army. One major was a sod, to put it mildly. We were on a train with flat trucks, in North Africa, sitting with our legs dangling down. They said, "Go on, kick him in the back". Someone did and off he went and he was never seen again. When we got back we all kept our mouths shut, we never said anything.

I was nearly taken prisoner. I wandered into the wrong camp one night. It was pitch dark and I had to deliver a dispatch. You used to find your way by the stars, but there was an easier way used by Headquarters. They used to lay wires straight out across the sand to the next camp, there could be many wires, they were tagged, you just followed the wire. Well, this night I was following the wire when they went underground because they crossed a tank track and then I lost my wire. I took what I thought was the right one, but it went into the Italian camp, I heard them talking and I turned and ran.

In the desert we used to have to carry the water 200 miles. We were only allowed one pint each a day. We could do what we wanted with it, wash, shave or drink it. Men went mad for water, some gulped it all down in one go. It was hot, 130 degrees in the shade. One day the sergeant from Stowmarket said I was getting transferred. He said, "Get your kit". We were on the move. I missed my water rations, because when we got to where we were going the water had been locked up. I was desperate so I went to the lorry radiator and let the water out and drank that, I wasn't ill, it was black. Some men went mad for water. We had to go on a 25 mile march and we weren't allowed to touch our pint. My word, there was trouble if you touched it, it was inspected at the end. Your feet were white with perspiration in the boots. For 18 months we never saw anyone, only soldiers. Hadn't seen a woman, the first we saw were dressed in black and looked awful. Our first sight of civilisation was telegraph poles, I remember that well.

One of my water trips was with the water cart, which was over 200 miles away. More men kept coming from all directions across the desert to get this water. Well, someone complained that the water wasn't fit to drink. Anyway, they lowered someone down the well and they found three bodies. They turned out to be three Australian women who were prostitutes brought in for the Italian officers to use, and they had been murdered and thrown down the well. The mirages were the worst thing especially when you were feeling thirsty. They make you even worse. You keep thinking you can see water and you go after it and then there's nothing there, drives you crazy.

This was in Tripoli in North Africa. Sometimes we were stationed for weeks on end in one place, everything was quiet. Suddenly a signal would come through, we had to pack up our kits, throw them on the lorries and go off, tracking further and further into the desert. One day on the road, it was covered in dust, I don't know how they could read the maps, there were four of us in a lorry. We broke down and the rest had to keep going. We lost contact with them altogether, but we had plenty of water in a big barrel but no food. In fact we had the others' water on our truck. I think we had a small tin of sardines between the four of us and one large 'dog' biscuit. We were lost for days. We repaired the truck and we just went round and round in circles. We eventually bumped into someone and found our way back to camp. We had to pick our track through the sand, we would sink down into the sand and have to lay down trays, long metal strips six-feet long, under the wheels, drive on then pick them up, then we'd get stuck again.

There were 300 men in the camp – all in tents. Supplies would be brought out to us. Petrol would be put in tins, like biscuit tins, packed in the lorry with straw in between to absorb the rough ride, of course the tins leaked like mad. It was dangerous with the straw. One in four tins was empty when they got to camp. The bottom of the truck would be soaked with petrol. We were very short of food. We heard little bits about the war on the radio. German planes would let out thousands of propaganda leaflets, which said, "Why carry on when your wives are at home carrying on with the Yanks?". Some men went berserk, one or two shot themselves. Life was not your own, you were like a prisoner, no freedom, you were just told to do everything and you just had to do it. The men had lots of fights, they played football to stop the boredom.

One day we were in camp and were very short of water, so I took a petrol can and thought if I walked a bit I must find something. The sand dunes were very high and I had gone to the top and walked about two miles and was just going back to camp when this army vehicle came charging towards me from nowhere. It was a German one, it pulled up alongside me, I was petrified, all I had was a petrol can and they were armed. A brigadier got out, then another officer and four men, they were all badly wounded. There was blood every-where and they just wanted to surrender, they were armed but not aggressive. I brought them back into camp with me. You should have seen the men's faces, they couldn't believe what they saw. I handed the men over to the field hospital and they were taken off somewhere as P.O.W. This was the battle of El-Alamein – started in Egypt and then went across the North of Africa.

From there we went off to Italy, we sailed from Tripoli to Salerno in southern Italy. It was there that Daisy's Gooderham's husband (I have heard that his name was Reg but not sure) got killed. I met up with him the day before for the first time. I thought I knew where he was so I went to the Headquarters to look up the map and then I set off to try to find him. I hitchhiked and eventually got there, he was looking after the P.O.W. camp. We had a good time, we ate a round of bread and jam and cups of tea and had a chat. I couldn't stop with him long because I had to get back. I told him I was going to Italy tomorrow and he said that he was too. Anyway, I heard that he was killed in a gun position. They were mortar shellings trying to get the range right. If the first was too short they'd lift the barrel and aim for a direct hit, he wouldn't leave the position and he got blown up. They even charged you for the blanket you were buried in.

Once in Italy the supplies had to be brought in. Petrol was always the most important. They laid a pipe, like a sewerage pipe along the top of the ground by the side of the road. Eventually it went from one end of the country to the other. You put a stand pipe on and pumped the petrol you wanted. I was there when Vesuvius went up, I was only half a mile away. For days it had kept smoking and spitting like fireworks. Everyone said that's not going to blow, it's been spitting for years. I was dishing out the food in the mess tent and up it went. Dust settled one foot thick over everything, road and rooftops. They had to get a bulldozer to push the grey ash off the roads, and they pushed it into the sea. Everywhere was dark for three days, no sun at all. When the lava came down we got out of its way and moved camp; it set like rock.

We gradually made our way up through Italy. Sometimes we were able to advance forward, sometimes we were driven back, sometimes it was all quiet for weeks. It was then that I would worry about how I was going to get home. When the war was over there were big celebrations but we still had not finished. When I was allowed home it took eight days. I hitchhiked on a lorry through Northern Italy, Germany, Switzerland, Austria and France. I got home in June 1946 and I went out in April 1940. When we came out of the Army it must have been like coming out of prison, where all your decisions had been made for you and suddenly you had to make your own decisions and you could do what you liked. How they decided who should come home was by the Captain taking a pack of cards – one was allowed to go. At first I couldn't, then it was my turn.

Some of the time I was attached to the American Army. Six of us had to go for six months. The Americans lived much better than us, they had plenty of food. In the canteen there was always a large box of chewing gum on top of a tea chest. The next one was full of sugar, next was full of cigarettes, we just had to help ourselves. This was every day, not just once in a while. When we were leaving the Sergeant came round and told us to walk round to his tent and said that we could take some cigarettes back for our men. We thought he meant a case but he meant a 1500 cwt truck full. We drove back several hundred miles to our camp, of course everyone was delighted. I was in the Signals, sending messages by morse code with a radio transmitter.

The first six months after I signed up we had to patrol the coast at Dymchurch in Kent. We would patrol the seafronts and one man would walk a mile, meet another soldier coming the other way, turn round and then walk back. The beach was all wired off, we were supposed to be looking for mines or for someone coming in by boat. One day, it just happened to be April 1st, it was in the early hours and dawn was just breaking, suddenly I saw this thing in the water. Christ, it was a mine! The waves were lashing it up the beach and back again. Any minute it was going to hit the sea wall. I rushed back to the hut sergeant and told him. He replied, "You won't catch me out son, I know it's April Fool's Day". Then there was an almighty bang as it hit the wall, it made a hole the size of a double-decker bus.

We had only one Spitfire patrolling the coast. I really think that the Germans made a mistake going after Russia first. If they had come over to us we would not have stood a chance. We had no weapons or ammunition when I was called up in Bury. They gave me an old rifle they took out of the Keep, it was so dirty it took me weeks to clean it. Eventually we were told to evacuate to Dunkirk and they gave me five rounds of ammunition. I never knew how to even load the gun, let alone use it.

It was just luck where you were sent. When we were at Ipswich I was lucky to get embarkations leave but my mates did not. They all went off to Singapore and got captured, and because I was later I went to Egypt. So it was just luck. I didn't want to collect my medals when I came home, but my mother insisted and she went and collected them for me.

Ron received the Italy Star, Africa Star – 1939-45 8th Army, the War Service Medal and an Italian Medal.

Olive Catchpole
3 Mount Close, Hessett

At Hessett School Mr Kent was the school teacher. He couldn't ever say the children's names properly. He would call me Glad-ice or El-anor (for Eleanor Mills) or Ol-live. He would say to me, "I owe you one". Perhaps I hadn't drawn a straight line or something and I would have to go out the front and get a ruler across my knuckles. Well, I remember Mrs Farley, we were all supposed to have our hands on our laps and we would have a ruler across our fingers if our hands were on the desk.

Olive in service: I was looking after a little boy at Thurston for a Mrs Carr and one day she said to me that she could no longer afford to keep me on. "Olive, we have got to let you go, I will do what I can to help you find another job". Well, one day Mrs Carr said to me, "Olive, put on your clean uniform. There is a lady down for the day from London and they might be able to give you a job". Anyway, I met them and they said that they would like to meet my parents. I was only about 13 or 14 then. When they got over to Drinkstone mother was out for a walk with the children and so they had a chat with father. He thought that it was a good idea but he wanted to lay down a few rules of his own. I was to be allowed to go to church and take Holy Communion. They said that was fine by them. When I left to go down to London I took with me an enormous bunch of cowslips. They came for me in the car and I went off with my tin trunk.

I was quite homesick at first, but I had some marvellous times, I went with the whole family to Wembley. This was about 1924. Mother came down to London to spend a few days with me. Mrs Haygate paid for us to take mother all over the place. When I first went to London I wore my "country boots" that had studs on the bottoms and didn't half rattle on the pavements. I felt so scared of slipping over. I felt out of it a bit because I did not have the right clothes. So the lady, Mrs Haygate, took me to Harrods to be kitted out. I had a tweed coat and hat, a walking out uniform, house shoes, under clothes, all on condition that I stayed in that employment. I got £8 a year then it went up to £10 and £12. The twins went to the Henrietta Barnett School in the Hampstead suburbs. When the daughter was 21 years her father bought her an Austin 7 car. He was quite wealthy, he used to buy estates and build houses. Some he had built in Hendon he named after some of our villages: Thurston, Beyton and Hessett. Mrs Haygate used to help him and she used to go to Rotterdam to buy some wood and timber. They had a house at Shoreham On Sea and if any of the children were ever ill they would all go down to the sea to recuperate. Once they all got whooping cough but they all got over it.

When father died, mother asked me if I could get a job nearer home but there were very few jobs available. Eventually I got a job as under maid at a big house in Garboldisham, I was 17 years old then. But it was back to hands and knees, no mod cons like I had in London. They had oak floors that had to be polished with beeswax and turpentine. I also cleaned all the brass and copper. I had to take a can of hot water upstairs to the bathroom every lunch time so they could wash before lunch. In the evening I changed into a black dress with a white apron. While they were upstairs washing I used to go into the drawing room and pump up the cushions and tidy up, put away the newspapers, do the pot plants and set the fire up and then when they went in there for the evening I went upstairs to tidy their bedrooms.

The head house maid looked after the mistress and I looked after Miss Rosemary. I used to have to put out her clothes for the next day. The girl, whose job I had, ended up with housemaid's knee, and I ended up with boils all over my arms. The lady said that I should see the doctor. Anyway, he said that he knew my mother and he had in fact brought me into the world. I was quite ill and was sent home and eventually I had my tonsils out when I was 18.

My son Bill and a little boy (John Gladwell - not sure if he was an evacuee, anyway he always had a runny nose), when they were about 11 years old they used to get up to all sorts of mischief. One day Mr Valentine said to me that he wanted to see them. So Bill went down the farm and he was gone ever such a long time. I was getting worried so I got on my bike and went down the lane to look for them. I saw Mr Valentine and he said not to worry and that he was dealing with it. It appeared that the boys had put some glass bottles on a fence and had thrown stones at them and the broken glass had fallen into the field where the cattle were. He told them that was the end of the matter provided they picked up the glass.

One day Maurice Cocksedge (Old Mr Cocksedge's son), he was a bit cheeky and a bit braver than the others, went to fish in Mr Squirrell's moat and he had been told not to. Anyway, he sat on the wall and Mr Squirrell crept up behind him and pushed him in with a hoe to teach him a lesson. One day when Bill and Johnny (Gladwell) came out of school they found that the church was unlocked. Well, they climbed up the steps of the tower to the top. When they came home for tea that night they happened to mention that there was a wonderful view and they could see all the way to Rougham. I said, "You've never been all the way up there?" I think the door of the tower has been locked ever since. The two boys always went missing, they used to go for miles some days. One day Bill had been swimming in the Mount moat and when he got in the bath his vest was on back to front and the water was yellow with mud!

To go to school the boys used to bike to Beyton, leave the bikes there and catch the 204 bus to Woolpit school. One day Bill and Johnny missed the bus and daren't go to school so they spent the day off on their bikes to Thurston to watch the trains at the station. They only had a few coppers so they bought a loaf of bread and a piece of cheese. Now the Attendance Officer (Mr Groves) was doing his rounds of the schools and had had lunch at Hessett and was then off to Woolpit. Of course the boys weren't there. Well I was preparing tea for my husband when there was a knock at the door and who should be standing there but the Attendance Officer. "Where's your Bill then?" I said he was at school, "Oh no he's not" – "Oh yes he is" and we went on like this. Well I read the riot act to him when he came home. And then another day when they missed the bus again they cycled all the way to Woolpit and got there just in time as Mr Groves was calling the register. "You have turned up then" he said. "Been watching the chuff chuffs?". I guess Bill would have just turned 12 by then.

Floods: I remember 1946 time when there were terrible floods down the street and John Cocksedge who lived down near the Black House got out a "Bungalow Bath" (a galvanized tin bath that took two children, one at each end). He attached two boards and rowed himself up to the shop.

Pub: The room at the left of the door as you go in the pub was always full of thick smoke. That's what I remember most when I was a child when I used to go and get some lemonade. All the old men used to gather in there and play dominoes. Ernie Frost's father was a verger at the church. His name was Ted Frost and he lived in one of the seven cottages which made up Five Bells Cottage opposite the pub.

Poker and Punch Green had been drinking one night and when they came out of the pub the moon was shining and reflecting in the puddle, so the moon looked as though it was in the puddle. They walked round and round and couldn't understand it. We used to take Punch home in the cart that they used to carry the electric poles when they were putting electricity into the village. There was the story of the man who when he came out of the pub, the shafts of his cart had been put through the gate railings and his horse attached again. Well he used to sell dried fish, herrings and bloaters. He always went into the pub for a drink.

At Lane Farm House, Mrs Woodard lived in one end, she also lived at Elm Farm once. Mr Goddard used to live in the old house at the back of the junction at the end of Hubbards Lane. The old orchard used to be full of fruit any time of the year; apples, pears and cherries, it was a wild place and we used to go up there as kids.

Coronation Day was celebrated on the field in front of Mr Mitcham's behind the chestnut trees. I remember that it was a very wet day. There were races for the children and refreshments and each child received a Coronation mug and some balloons.

I remember that during the war when the Americans were at Rougham they used to come over to see us in the village. One evening a buzz bomb (V1) came over and we just stood there watching it. The Americans shouted to us, "Get inside you crazy Limeys". My sister's boyfriend was here one evening and when he came over he said in his loudest voice, "Praise the Lord and keep the "B" going". I remember once he came over one Sunday evening and my neighbour was in the Home Defence at the Bury Barracks. His wife had just said goodbye to him as he was cycling back to Bury and she had her curlers in ready for bed when one came over so low. Well, she leaped over the top of the hedge to ours she was so frightened. It was so low bricks vibrated off the chimney and rolled down the thatch. It came down in the wood after the engine cut out and then crashed. It had hit a tree in Drinkstone Park before it landed over there so you could tell how low it was. Of course the next day the children all went over to bring back souvenirs. The more the Germans came through France, the further inland here they were able to send the buzz bombs.

VE Day: It was a lovely feeling of relief when we knew that there would be no more Germans sending any more bombs. We could go to bed each night in peace. I am not sure we celebrated much in Hessett. It was just another day, it wasn't the end of the war. I think they celebrated more in the towns. We probably had a church service of thanksgiving. But one celebration I remember was a fancy dress on the meadow behind the trees. I told my husband I was going to enter. "Don't you show yourself off like that", he said. I said that I was going as Mrs Mop. I wore a black dress and apron, black shoes and stockings and a mop and bucket. Well, Brig. Daniels of Hessett House was one of the judges. I thought I'd have a bit of fun so I walked up to him and said, "Can I do you now, Sir". Well, you should have seen his face, he was not amused. The event was probably raising money for the Salute the Soldier campaign.

During the war my husband's cousin Rosie was living with us and perhaps you would go down to the village hall of an evening. When we were walking home and it was a moonlit night Rosie would say, "I hope mum and dad are alright in London", and if it was a cloudy night she would say, "Thank God".

I remember one day I had taken our youngest son Bill down to the school to be immunised against whooping cough and when we were walking home there was a funny sound coming from behind the trees. Suddenly there was a plane that emerged from over the trees and I could see two men in the front of the plane, and the plane had a swastika on the side. It was a German plane. Well, we took to our heels with the prams and raced up the road to the house. The plane dropped a bomb in the beet factory lagoon, and it was cheeky enough to fly over us on its way back but I don't think it got much further before it was shot down. In the Summer we had double summertime and it was light really late into the evening. Cliff always walked round the garden last thing at night before he went to bed. He was watching to see if any buzz bombs were coming.

Mr Snelling had a taxi in Rattlesden and there was great competition between him and the carrier in Hessett who used a horse and cart. Mr Sturgeon lived in the house next door to Mr Mill's shop and he used to take people into Bury every market day with the open cart. The cart used to hold about 20 people and if it was raining everyone used to have their umbrellas up. Others would give him a shopping list and he would bring things back for them. He kept his horse in the field at the back of his house. I always remember going in with mother on market day. We would pack some bread and butter and then buy some fish and chips and take them into the Abbey Gardens to eat them. I remember that it used to cost 1/2d to go to Bury when the buses came in. When father had his harvest bonus we all used to go into Bury to buy boots for the winter. We couldn't buy them very often and they got repaired a lot and taken to the shoe mender who lived at Vine Cottage.

First Drinkstone Guides: I remember that the Guides used to meet in the ballroom at the old Drinkstone Hall in the park. The floor was covered with long strips of material for the carpet and we were not allowed to wear our outside boots. The Guide Captain said to me, "Olive, have you any other shoes you can wear?" and of course I said that I had not. "Well", she said, "I'll see what I can do". Anyway she brought a pair of her mother's. They were beautiful shoes with a French heel and made of kid leather. They made my toes hurt but I felt so important. In those days every Guide troop did something special like country dancing. Drinkstone troop were noted for our marching. Major Crow had married Miss Hargraeves from the Hall, and he brought a portable gramophone and put it on the card table and played military marching music. Well, we marched and marched and did wheels and things. My father also helped as he was a Company Sergeant Major in the First World War. Before I went each week I had to parade in front of my father to make sure that my shoes were polished and I looked smart in my uniform. Of course, I was Olive Blake then and I think Ivy Pool was also there at the same time.

Miss Hargreaves wanted to have a library for the Guides at Drinkstone Hall and she asked us all to help collect the books. She asked me to help sort them and classify them. There was one book by Angela Brazil that I remember well. One day my father said to me, "Olive, do you think that there are any books that I could read?" Well, I chose for him a book called 'Under the Red Robe' by Stanley Weyman, all about the French Revolution. So I took it to the Captain to be stamped. "Why, Olive is your father fond of reading?" she said, "I'll see if I can find him some more". After that there were piles of the Punch Magazine put aside for him and the Strand Magazine. One day I was in the front room and I was giggling about a story I was reading. There was a lady who had been to church that morning when the vicar had been complaining about the "commentators". She thought he was complaining about the "common taters" and she didn't agree with him. So the next day she went round to the Rectory and said "Please Sir, I have brought you a bag of my red common taters, they really are very nice".

We had a concert at school one day and the Rev. Bartlett came to watch the rehearsals. We were reciting the poem – "Twas the night before Christmas", when we came to the bit where we had to say, "He had a broad face and a little round belly that shook when he laughed and looked just like some jelly", Well the Rev. didn't think that this was appropriate and he tried to think of something else but he couldn't so the words had to stay.

Ivy Pool lived near the Reading Room. We had concert parties and the political parties held their meeting there. There was a man who used to come from Bury, he was a female impersonator. Newspapers from the Rectory would be sent down for the men to read and the men would play billiards. The ladies were not allowed in. The Rector's wife held sewing parties where the women used to meet. They would save what coppers they could afford and when they had enough they would go on outings. At certain times of the year my mother used to go to Bury to buy grey calico and she used to make sheets and chemises, night dresses and knickers. After the First World War mother brought a sewing machine and she did the larger work and I did the finishing off by hand and do the feather stitching. At first the clothes used to be very scratchy but after they had been boiled a few times they were quite comfortable to wear.

On Sunday mornings Mrs Halls who lived at the Guildhall took Sunday School in the Reading Room. The Rector came in before 11am to take the prayers and we would all troop up to the church. All the children would sit in front of Mrs Frost's father who was the verger. Then the service used to start but the children would go out before the sermon began. On Sunday afternoons there was a children's service and we were given texts to collect if you attended and then we were given prizes for good attendance. You know that we had some wall paintings on the church walls, well the Rev. Bartlett used to tell us about them and he made them sound so interesting. After tea we would go back to the church and I would sing in the choir.

When we had moved to Drinkstone and I had to practise for the Lent service at Easter mother used to let me walk through the footpath at the back of the church across the Park, we had to go through about three kissing gates. I always remembered the tune. In recent years we had a Christmas party in the village hall and one year the St. Mary's Hand Bells came and to my amazement started to play that tune. When they had finished I said, "Excuse me, what was that piece of music?" It was called "Evening Hymn".

Drinkstone School: When I was at Drinkstone school we used to go to Woolpit for cookery lessons. We walked across the fields. We had a proper range there to learn on, just plain cooking and we had monitors for the cookery lessons.

Aggie Worley (nee Green)
Shangri-la, The Heath, Hessett

Aggie Worley lived with her family in one side of a cottage that had been built on the site of the ruins of Old Hessett Hall. Her grandmother, Elizabeth Green, lived in the other side of the same cottage.

To reach the cottage you had to walk over a slatted wooden bridge which spanned the deep moat that surrounded the site. The moat went all the way round. It used to get frozen over every winter so father and my uncles from next door used to stand on the ice and trim back the big hedge in the front. We used to have lots of fun sliding around on the ice with the other children from the village, but my aunt, who was only a few years older than me, drowned one day in the moat. When I was born I was named after her – Agnes. To get to our cottage we used to use the gate across the meadow – the one that is in the corner of Old Hall Road (Heath Road). The Old Hall Road was made of gravel, it was not made of tarmac, when I was a child.

There were three bedrooms in grandmother's cottage and two in ours. I remember the boys slept on mattresses on the floor and the girls had the beds. Grandmother, Elizabeth Green, had 13 children – three girls and the rest were boys. I remember that there was a well outside and the garden was full of fruit trees of all sorts, greengages, plums, damsons, apples and pears. Mother made her own bread in a big faggot oven twice a week and she used to make us tiny little cottage loaves. She would get the yeast from the bakers at Rougham. Mum used to make pork cheeses, sausages and brawn. A brawn is when the meat is all shredded up and set in a kind of jelly made from the juices and put in a basin to set. Then it was cut with a knife and we had it for our tea, it was delicious. As a child we had porridge for breakfast and we often did toast on a toasting fork.

Mother worked up at the Rectory for the Rev. Bartlett. When I went to school I wore a gym slip that the rector's wife had given mother. I was the only one wearing one and I felt so important. I didn't half fancy myself. I mostly had my aunt's clothes handed down to me. Once I remember her white washing the walls of the kitchen and then making a pretty pattern by pressing on the blue bag to make a lovely pattern on the wall. I think that grandfather, Jacob

Green, worked on the farm or up at the fruit farm at Beyton. I know my Uncle Walter Green and Uncle Herbie (Herbert) Green worked at the fruit farm. They were two of our World War 1 casualties. As children we used to run to the gate when they came back from work as they always brought us an apple.

My father, Manasseh Green, worked for Fred Squirrell up at Spring Farm, he was the horseman there. I can remember having to take his "fourses" up to the fields at teatime during the harvest. They would have an earthenware jug full of beer and some hot tea that we took in an enamel jug with some bread and cheese and cakes that mother had made. We would follow the wagon back to the farm and then have a ride back to the fields. I was allowed to ride on one of the old horses named "Old Charlie", he was very quiet. They then cut the corn with a binder. We had fun chasing the rabbits and they often gave us one to take home for tea. When father left for work in the morning he used to take his "elevenses" with him wrapped up in a cloth bag. After their "fourses" they would then work on till late. I was about seven when my father died.

I don't remember any of the ruins of the Old Hall but father had built pig sties and chicken runs there and I can remember the rats – hundreds of them. I can remember the chickens and the ducks and you could walk right into the moat.

About the time Grandmother married and moved to Derbyshire we moved down to the cottages at the Wash (down by the Old School). Mr Sturgeon owned these cottages. But after a few years he put the rents up and mother couldn't afford to stay so she moved up to the Heath in the row of cottages that got burnt down. Mr Austin owned these. My mother died in 1939.

Rev. Bartlett was the Rector when I was at school, I can remember Sunday School treats at the Rectory when we went up there for tea. We had lots of fun swinging from the trees in the drive way. I was also in the choir with a girl called Audrey, Nellie Sturgeon and Lilly Sturgeon. My brother used to pump up the bellows for the organ in the church. The old Reading Room was where the village hall is now. It was an old tin shed with a galvanised tin roof.

When I was at school we used to walk to Rougham for our cookery lessons. We would either walk or bike there. The boys stayed in the school at Hessett for carpentry lessons and gardening on their patch of ground. Mrs Halls was my teacher, she lived in the Guildhall. Her husband, Lawton Halls, was a general builder and he used to make coffins in his workshop.

I remember when I was a child we would go to Bury on a Wednesday in the carriers cart. There would be great excitement that day, if it was raining we covered our legs with a tarpaulin. The cart could carry six people and you would have to book the seats. It cost 1/6d for adults and 9d for the children. Mr Sturgeon would set off in the morning at about 9am and we would meet other carts on the road and lots of people on bicycles, lots of people cycled to Bury in those days. He used to put the cart in the pub yard in Bury and then we would come away home at about 4pm.

We would mostly just go for shoes because we had a good grocers shop in the village run by Mr Mills, and he would always get anything that you wanted. Mr Mills used to make his own bread and bread also came from the baker at Rougham from the Lion Yard opposite the Bennett Arms. Mr Lambert from Hurdle Cottage used to make hurdles next door to the timber yard.

I used to work for a Mr Earith in Quaker Lane where Ray Rogers used to live. Then I worked in Hampshire for a Miss Powell, the sister of Lord Baden Powell. I also worked at the Red Cross at the Rougham Aerodrome. We used to get the sandwiches ready for the pilots when they flew home. We used to count the planes and knew if some had got shot down. I worked there from 1pm until 10pm in the canteen. The Americans had crates of oranges and butter and lots of cigarettes. They used to give me candy for my son Derek, I got to know all the boys very well.

I can remember the day of the fire when the second row of cottages burnt down. It was after the war and I was in Bridge Cottage and I can remember my cousin came running out of the house where May Cottage in Heath Road is now and said to me that the thatch was on fire but I said that I couldn't come now because I had a sponge in the oven and I would come presently. It was Florence Costello's house and they got all her furniture out onto the garden and Dick Renson came up with his lorry and took it all down to the Reading Room for safe keeping. I think Florence went to stay with Mr and Mrs Mills. The fire engines came but they couldn't do much to save the row of cottages.

Mother always used to do the baking on Saturdays – all the cakes and the sausage rolls. Monday was always wash day and all the water had to come up from the well and be put in the water butt. My husband, Alfred William Worley, used to do that on Sunday evenings ready for Monday, and then we would do the ironing on the Tuesday.

Paul Catchpole
2nd November 1994

Mr Snell lived at Hill Farm. He was the Scout master during the war days and the Scouts met at the Mission Hall.

We use to get the old fuel tanks off the fighter planes at the dump. It would take three of us to carry them. We'd cut a hole in them and use them as a boat. Dad said that it would tip over so we filled it with stones but it still tipped over.

We used to play on the Mount, there was water in the moat then. As children we would gather wild raspberries and strawberries over in the woods. The Americans would give us a 3d bit (just over 1p) for them and we were thrilled.

Major Fairbrother lived in Quaker Lane. He was a typical major in the army. I remember one day when the street was flooded and he drove up in his Bullnose Morris car, got out and looked at the depth of the water. He wasn't going to be put off so he marched through the flood water to the shop and came out and drove off again, nothing was going to stop him. He said this was nothing compared with the desert (1946).

There is a spring somewhere down at the ford we used to call Johnny's hole. It was crystal clear. Mrs Gant used to get the water from there to do her washing she took in. She also washed the surplices for the church.

Mr Kent the school master had a dreadful habit of coming up behind you and putting both of his fists on your shoulder bones at the back and shake you. Mr Kent had a motor bike and side car and when it wouldn't start he would expect us boys to push him. Well, we'd push him up the verge into the hedge.

Hub Sturgeon repaired wagon wheels up at the corner of the green. When I came out of school I used to go and help him; I expect that I was more of a hindrance than help.

My father was a horseman for Mr Hargraves at Drinkstone, and I remember taking a bottle of cold tea with no milk, some bread and cheese to him in the fields.

Arthur Bloomfield
23 April 2007

Arthur came to Hessett from Tostock when he was six years of age and had lived in the village all his life. He attended the school and after leaving worked on the land for the Agnew Estate.

The family lived in a row of cottages more or less where Renson Close is now. When those cottages were pulled down the family moved to new houses built in Heath Road, and later Arthur moved to Mount Close where he lived for the rest of his life.

One of the jobs he had to do was clear out the ditches, making them ready for the winter weather, and he mainly worked on his own. Below is an insight into the agricultural labourer's work schedule, month by month.

January
The slackest time of the year. The stock is the main work, feeding and bedding, with hedging and ditching filling in the time. The threshing machine would come to thresh the last of the corn stacks.

February
Usually in the third week of February, as soon as the fields were dry enough, drilling would start with beans and peas.

March
As it got warmer wheat, barley and oats would be drilled, followed by sugar beet.

April
The rest of the sugar beet was drilled and the stock were put out to graze. When the fields were dry enough winter corn was rolled and top dressed, some were harrowed to kill the weeds as there were no sprays then.

May
As spring corn came through it would be rolled and as the sugar beet came up it would be horse hoed ready for hand hoeing.

June
Hand hoeing and horse hoeing would continue through the month and some of the sugar beet would go for silaging.

July
Cutting hay would mean lots of work turning it to dry. They would turn it by hand and leave for several days before carting and stacking. The sugar beet would be second hoed before they would horse hoe for the last time.

August
Cutting corn would start about the second week with a binder. The sheaves would be shocked (group of sheaves of grain). The shocks would be left on the field until dry enough to cart and stack. The oats stayed on the fields for three Sundays.

September
Corn carting was the main work when dry enough. The next job was to clean out the stock yards and put the muck on the fields before they started to plough and drill. Sugar beet lifting could start if other work allowed.

October
The main work was lifting, pulling, topping and carting sugar beet. The lifting and carting was done by horses, the pulling and topping was done by hand. The mangolds (a large kind of beet grown for cattle fodder) would be topped and clamped before they were frozen.

November
Beeting and ploughing was the main thing before the bad weather set in. They would thresh one or two corn stacks for feeding and bedding before the stock came in for winter.

December
With beeting and ploughing coming to an end, the main threshing and chaff cutting for feeding and bedding was the last thing before Christmas and the start of a new year.

Harvest time: Left to right, Fred Bullett, Harry Cocksedge, Ray Rogers on the tractor, Ivan Rogers, Bill Davies and Herbie Bullett.

George Bullett with a horse called Dodman and Sid Bullett with Smart at Hall Lane.

Elizabeth Nicholson (nee Valentine)
2nd March, 2008

My parents, Edna and Norman Valentine, were newly married and took over Lane Farm in Hubbards Lane in 1945. Life was very hard for them in the early days as the farmhouse was in a poor condition with no electricity or running water, and it was very damp and draughty. There were plenty of mice in the attic and, what seemed to me as a child, hundreds of chirping sparrows in the thatch. The water came from a well outside and the toilet was in a shed at the end of the vegetable garden.

In the kitchen was a large black range with a bread oven and a copper for heating hot water at one end. The floor was made of large uneven flag stones and the walls were whitewashed. There was a pantry and gun room off to the right. To the left was a parlour and a sitting room with a latched door which led up to the three bedrooms with sloping ceilings in the roof space, they all led into each other. The bedrooms were very cold in the winter with ice patterns forming on the windows overnight but cool under the thatch in the summer. To the right of the stairs there were two other attic rooms which were not used.

By the 1950s electricity must have come to the houses down the lane and a pump was put in the well and then father built a kitchen and inside bathroom with a flat roof at the back. In the 1960s the thatch was in such a poor state that the house was pulled down before it fell down and a new house built on the same site. I remember that we had use of the downstairs rooms while the upper floors and the roof were built round us. We had really warm summers in those days as I remember well sleeping in a large marquee on the front garden for many weeks with my brother and sister whilst the work was completed. It was good fun for us as children except if you stood on a hedgehog that had crept in over night!

After the war it was a new age in farming for all things mechanical to the demise of the working farm horse. My father's first tractor was a little grey Massey Ferguson, now an icon in the farming world, and he then designed in 1947 and built a mechanical sugar beet hoe which worked from the back of the tractor. It is now featured on the Hessett village sign and known locally as the "Valentine Hoe". It was quite revolutionary at the time as previously the work had to be done by hand. Several of these machines were manufactured by Messrs Fiddlers Ltd of Stowmarket.

Mr parents continued to make a small living off the land, growing cereals and sugar beet with a small herd of Ayrshire cows and I can remember the milk lorry clattering down the lane each morning to collect the three or four churns of milk. Unfortunately, most of the herd died of 'bloat' when they had wandered off into a clover field one day. The rich clover had fermented in their stomachs. We also had a flock of laying hens and a small herd of Large White pigs, but these also succumbed to Fowl Pest and Swine Fever in the 1960s.

In the late 1950s and early 1960s one of the fields was excavated for hoggin. Hoggin is a mixture of sand, gravel and flint and was used to extend the runways at RAF Lakenheath and RAF Mildenhall. It left a very large deep pit in the field but now we know it as a beautiful lake and nature reserve.

There was also another cottage at the end of the lane, nearer to Drinkstone Lane, no longer there, known as Barbers Cottage belonging to the Gamekeeper for the Drinkstone Estate. The field nearby was called Barbers Field. All the fields down the lane had their own names. In the 1980s the old poultry sheds at Lane Farm were converted into a meat processing factory and then in 1990 the Bovis homes were built.

My father was also a Hessett Parish Councillor for many years and a member of the old Thedwastre Rural District Council. My mother taught for many years at the Convent School and South Lee School in Bury St Edmunds. I had a very happy childhood living 'down the lane'. My brother, sister and I had to work hard on the farm but we had happy times with our ponies, climbing trees in the orchard, making camps and generally making our own amusements.

My most vivid memories now are the wildlife we lived alongside. The hundreds of sandmartins that nested in the steep sides of the pit after the excavation of the hoggin, the carpets of primroses and cowslips in the ditches around the fields and the badgers that lived under the old holly tree.

Susan Tipple and Ann Rose (nee Frost)
16th June, 2008

Susan Tipple, who has lived in Hessett all her life apart from a year when she was newly married, remembers with Ann Rose growing up in the village.

My parents were Ernie and Alice Frost and living in one of the houses on The Green. I was one of 10 children and because we needed more rooms we then moved to one of the houses at Manor Road on the way to Felsham at the end of the village. On Sunday we went to Sunday School in the Village Hall and then on to church to sing in the choir. We sang and Mrs Dolly Bauly played the organ.

Mr Frost worked at the iron foundry in Stowmarket and would cycle down to Beyton to catch the bus. When he came home one evening his bike had gone; it was found in the pond in Quaker Lane. We also went to the iron foundry at Christmas time when they had a party for the workers' children and we were given big bars of chocolate. Mrs Frost had a job helping Mrs Valentine at Lane Farm, and she was also churchwarden for twenty-four years.

I started school in Hessett, the teachers name was Mrs Farley and she was very strict. There was a big fireguard around the fire which the door was always kept shut. In the winter when it was cold the milk defrosted beside the fire. Mrs Farley wore long brown leather lace up boots.

One day we played rounders on the field which adjoined the playground and the ball went into a garden of a nearby cottage, of which there were four together. We were frightened of the lady who lived there and nobody would go and get the ball. My nephew and I ran to the allotments and hid in the cabbage patch. The landlady of the Five Bells Inn, Mrs Medcalf, saw us and at the same time the school inspector, Mr Groves, arrived and Mrs Medcalf told where we were so Mr Groves came and got us. Mother was informed and we both had sore behinds for a few days. I cannot remember the name of the lady, but Mrs Daphne Harris and Mrs Ella Pearson lived in two of the cottages.

On Boxing Day we would go to our grandparents' house in Rougham, where we would have lunch and tea. Because there were 10 children, and we had no transport, we had some being pushed in the pram, some walking and some on bikes, and then we had to come home to Hessett in the dark. When Hessett School closed we were taken by a Mulley's bus, the driver's name was Dennis, to Drinkstone School. The teachers name there was Mrs Collins. My job was to take Mrs Collins' dogs for a walk, so my mother went to the school as I was not learning any lessons. We stayed at Drinkstone until it was time to go to Beyton School.

We would bike to Beyton and Mr Cockell would pick my brother John up as he had a bad leg and there was a bus that came by but did not always stop and pick him up. We would bike home at lunch time and back again for the afternoon classes. If you had a puncture coming home at lunch time you would have to walk home and then back to school and had to mend the puncture that evening.

Once home from school we all had our jobs to do around the house and they had to be done before we were allowed out to play. We had to bring in the coal, chop the firewood, and scrub the table. Dad had an allotment and we had to collect the potatoes and vegetables before they could be got ready for the next day.

At the end of the garden was the wash house where the washing was done in a big copper boiler every Monday and Friday, which we also had to help with. Next to the wash house was the toilet. It was not very nice going down to the end of the garden in the middle of the night, and every so often dad would have to empty the bucket, he would dig a hole and bury the contents. Then next to that was the coal bunker where we had to get the coal from, rain or shine.

In the summer at harvest time the children would help and go into the fields with sticks to try and capture the rabbits. Dad would take us to Monk Wood, which was up Hubbards Lane and down the right hand track and the wood was on the left hand side. We would pick up sticks for the beans and peas. During the evenings, weekends and school holidays the children would play on The Green; there would be rounders, cricket and other games. There was never any arguing when everyone was playing the different games, and there was also a youth club held in the old village hall. When called to go in, if we did not want to, we would hide in the ditch. In the ditch we had corrugated iron sheets placed over the top and covered with soil and grass, it was a good place to hide. We also made a den in the ditch on The Green the Heath Road side. As we got older and in our teens we had to be in by 10pm. I (Susan) can remember getting 6d (2½ p) for combing dad's hair as he was bald on the top and I used to comb the side hair up over his head to cover the bald patch. Mum had a gate up to keep the younger children in, and she said I should have been a boy, as I would get a chair up to the gate, climb on the chair and then climb over the gate.

The shopping was delivered from the International Stores in Bury, and the driver's name was Les. He would deliver on Wednesday and take the book for the next week's delivery. When we cleared out the kitchen draws we found the order book and all the receipts. Mum also shopped at Mr Mills shop in the village.

My sister Ann worked at Mr Mills' shop and one year she brought some fireworks home and there was a jumping jack, which we decided to light in our bedroom, which was at the back of the house. We had a lovely brass bed. Anyway, we lit the firework and tried to throw it out of the window, but it missed and came back in and was jumping all over the floor. We both got a smack with the wooden spoon. Mum would buy our clothes with some being made, my sister had a pair of shoes which I loved, when they got my size I had them, and when they were getting too small for me my mum cut the toe area out so I had peep-hole shoes.

When my brother Ray and Ann got married, I and Susan were bridesmaids and had my hair permed especially for the day. I had always wanted curly hair so I combed it so much that it started to fall out.

I remember when a row of houses up the Heath caught fire. Ann had got John on the back of the bike, I ran by the side. The fire engine passed and then a police car. The police car stopped and told us not to have two people on a bike, so John got off but as soon as they had gone he got back on again. The cottage had caught fire from a spark from one of the houses in the other row. There were four cottages there; we can only remember three of the names: Mrs Williams, Mrs Everett and Mrs Costello. They had to sleep in the Village Hall until they were rehoused.

Coming down the Heath one day I found a moorhen's nest which had eggs in so I decided to bring them home and put them in a box where mum had got a hen. So I took the hen's eggs out and put the moorhen's eggs in and three or four days later all these baby moorhens hatched, my mum was not very pleased.

I would chase my sister round the garden with a chicken as she did not like any feathered animals. Mum had geese in the field behind Shrubbery Farm and would chase the children that ventured into the field.

Other things that we had in Hessett: there was a fete at Hessett House where Mr and Mrs Daniels lived, I was an ice cream girl and had a dress of crepe paper in the colours of strawberry, vanilla and chocolate made by my mum. We also had a bonfire in November on the village green when we had fireworks. Then at Christmas we went carol singing around the villages, we also had a Sunday School Christmas party and I can remember the Rev. Matthews had a faith healing service at the church where people would go up to be blessed and healed.

Peter Cornish
8th November, 2008

My mother, Florence Bullett, and father, Harry Cornish, married and lived where Mount Close is now. There was a group of three cottages and two cottages and they lived in one of the two cottages. My brother and I were born there and I have lived in the village all my life. In those days the coal was delivered from Peaches Yard at Thurston and milk came from Shrubbery Farm where Mr Bauly lived. I would take the jug with a lid and collect the milk when I came home from school. My father would collect the water daily for the family from the well. My brother and I started school in the village, where The Old School House in Drinkstone Road now stands. There was a track running at the back of the school into what is now Drinkstone Road.

When the council houses in Beyton Road were built in 1952 the family moved from the cottage, into a new house. The teachers' names were Mrs Halls, who taught in the little room, and Mrs Farley who taught in the other room and was rather strict. Mrs Hall used to stand in front of the fire to warm herself while the children were told to get on with what they were doing. She had long bloomers that came down to her knees, which we could see when she held her skirt up to warm her legs! We would work on the school garden, where Holly House now stands, and we planted crops and sold the vegetables we grew for the school. Once or twice a week Mr Creed came over and showed us what to do.

Mr Groves, the attendance officer, would come round and check the register to see who was missing or had not been to school. We also had the nurse who came to look at our heads to see if we had any nits, and then the dentist would come to look at our teeth to see if any were bad. If you did have a bad tooth they gave you an injection and you had it taken out there and then. We also had a doctor come round to see if we were healthy and had no problems. When I was seven Arthur Blomfield and I were sliding down Mr Bauly's haystack and I fell and broke my collar bone. Dr. Stevens put it in sticky plaster and when it came to have the plaster off, as I did not make a noise, he gave me 2d as a reward.

When I was at school I joined the Scouts which met in the Scout Hut which was joined to the Church Room. You went into the hall and then went into the Scout Hall by a door half way down the room.

While at school my uncle Fred, who worked for Mr Squirrell at Spring Farm, put some muck in my boots one day and said it would make me grow, so I went home to mother and asked if I had grown. She asked why, so I told her what they had done.

I left school when I was 14 and went to work at Woolpit for the sand and gravel company and I was there for two years. My wages were 25 shillings a week (£1-25p), and because I did my work properly he gave me a rise of 2/6d (13½ p). My father bought me a bike, which I had to pay him back out of my wages every week. I had to bike to work in all weathers and I can remember trying to keep it clean. Once while cycling to work I was trying to clean the spokes with a piece of rag which got caught in the wheel and I fell off and cut all my knees.

When Uncle Fred took over Nether Street Farm, Rougham, I left the sand and gravel site and went to work for him. I worked on the farm for 18 years and then left and went to work on the Rougham Estate, working in the Forestry Department. I enjoyed working there and stayed until I retired. While working at Rougham I bought a motor bike, and several of my friends had motor bikes as well to get to work.

My mother did all her shopping in the shop at Hessett where you could buy everything, and she also went into Bury on a Wednesday or Saturday. The buses that came though Hessett during the week were one in the morning and one home at night, except Wednesday and Saturday when one came through mid morning to Bury and back mid afternoon, but there would be more buses through Beyton as it was on the main road.

When I was older I went to the public house, as you were not allowed near the pub until you were old enough, for if my father saw me near the pub I would get a smack and told to go home. Sometimes we would walk down to Beyton with mother, father and grandfather and sit outside the White Horse and have a drink.

During the war I can remember the tanks coming down the road and also the doodlebugs. These were unmanned aircraft packed with high explosives, used by the Germans during World War II. One day we were at the allotments on the grounds, where Lime Tree Close is now, when a doodlebug came over and we all jumped into the ditch. It landed near Freewood Farm in the woods. Coloured American servicemen were stationed in Drinkstone Park and would take the bombs which were kept there by lorry to the airfield at Rougham. The Five Bells at Hessett was barred to the white Americans as it was for the coloured Americans only.

On Sunday afternoons we would go into Bury by bus, which we would have to walk to Beyton to catch, and would go to the pictures. There were three picture houses in Bury; the Odeon, where the shopping arcade Cornhill Walk is now; the Central in Hatter Street; and the Playhouse around where Argos is now. The Playhouse also had a bar where you could get a drink afterwards and then catch the bus and walk from Beyton home.

When my mother and father passed away I applied to the council to take over the house and I was given permission to do so. I met my wife June when her family came for a drink at Hessett Bells. We married and have lived in the same house ever since.

Joan Brinkley (nee Renson)
8th October, 2009

I was born in Hessett in one of four thatched cottages, opposite Lime Tree Close, in the second one along from the Old Post Office and moved into a shop, Laurel Dene, when I was two. Dad worked driving a lorry, Mum would walk up to the shop to buy Dad`s cigarettes everyday. One evening she went and the people who were at the shop told Mum that they were moving, and said that the building belonged to two sisters named Mulley who lived in Tostock. So Mum had a word with Dad who got his bike out and rode over to Tostock, had a word with the sisters, made a deal and paid them a deposit and the building was theirs. Dad paid £140 in all.

The people who were renting Laurel Dene were named Cross. When we moved I would say, "I don't like being here, this belongs to Mrs Cross". I was about four at the time. Mum and Dad would laugh at me saying this is our home now and it belongs to us. Dad carried on working with the lorry and Mum ran the shop. Dad hired the land opposite to Laurel Dene and he kept pigs and chickens on it. When the baby chicks were born I would pick them up and would hold them a bit too tight. Mum kept the shop going and also did needlework. Before she married she was a lady's maid and made some curtains and covers for Beyton House. There was a gentleman living there, but I cannot remember his name.

I had a good childhood and went to the local school. We learnt gardening in the school grounds where Holly House is now standing, and went to Rougham school for cookery. Mrs Farley was the teacher and she was very nice. Hessett Street would get flooded from Laurel Dene right up to Beyton Road which meant we could not get to school, because the water was so high. The games we played were `five fingers`, I think it is called `jacks` now; we ran hoops along the road as there was not the traffic there is now, and we went to Spring Farm climbing on the machinery and getting oil on our clothes. We also played ball up against the Mission wall.

Vine Cottage used to be the cobblers shop where the shoes were made and mended. We would tie a piece of string onto his doorknocker and go into the meadow opposite, pull the string so that the doorknocker would bang. He would open the door and shout at us and called us `varmint's`. We would also walk down Hubbards Lane to the Keepers Cottage.

I was at school until I was 15. Dad did not want me to leave school but I found a job at Amos' opposite Beyton church. My wages were 4¾d (2p) an hour. Then I went to work for Mr Sharman, delivering the milk. We had two churns on the back of the van and out of a churn measured a pint of milk into jugs that the customers had brought with them. Everybody had milk delivered in those days. Mr Sharman taught me to drive when I worked on the milk round and was then driving every day.

I was in the choir at Hessett church and went every Sunday, I loved it. We had a lovely Rector called the Rev Morton Bartlett, what you would call a real parson in those days. I started to drive a car when I was 17 and the parson had a Rover car and took confirmation. On the day the children were due to be confirmed the parson could not go so he asked if I would drive his car to Great Ashfield. I drove the car and they were all confirmed by the vicar of Great Ashfield.

We used to go dancing a lot during the war. They had dances at Thurston and we would also go into Bury to the Co-op hall in Out Risbygate Street and the Athenaeum. There were a lot of RAF personnel from Honington and Polish airmen. We would bike everywhere. We also went to the pictures down Hatter Street and the cinema was called The Central. We would leave our bikes at Langton Garage, where Langton Place is now, in Hatter Street which closed at 10 o`clock. If we were late and the garage was closed we had to walk home along the old A45. If we were lucky we might get a lift. We also used to go pea picking to raise a little more money. My friend and I went one day and somebody took all the peas we had picked so we did not get paid, that was very annoying.

I was also a home help and looked after Mr Clarke's mother and father-in-law when he was living at Hessett House. They lived in the flat next door. We went into town by bus on Christmas Eve; we did all our shopping round the market, and managed to get all our presents and bits and pieces in that one day. When I married we lived in a bungalow along The Green. I delivered the papers to the houses in those days as the shop did not stock them.

Eric Wilding
November 2011

I have lived in Hessett all my life and was born in the house where Hurdle Cottage and May Cottage now stand. These were originally three cottages and we lived in the middle one which is now part of Hurdle Cottage. We had to go through the neighbours' path to get to the road. I went to Hessett School where there were two classrooms, Mrs Farley in the big room teaching the older children and Mrs Halls in the smaller room teaching the younger children. Mrs Halls also took the Sunday School.

We had a hand pump to get the water from the well and when that ran dry, we went to the well in my uncle's garden which never ran dry, however hot and long the summer was. My mother would shop at Mr Mill's shop in the village and if he hadn't got what you wanted in the morning, he would very often have it there for you in the evening. There was also a butchers van that came round on a Saturday run by Addisons of Woolpit. Along with my friends, we would often pick wild strawberries in the woods owned by Rougham Estate and were frequently chased off by Toby, the gamekeeper.

My grandfather lived at Felsham and he worked from 6am to 6 pm, six days a week, and also went to church on Sunday. They had Christmas Day off and were not paid for Boxing Day if they chose to have that day off too. When I left school at 14, I went to work on a farm at Beyton where I learnt to plough with horses. We liked to go to the pictures on Saturday and Sunday and called at the Bennet Arms in Rougham on the way home. We also went to the Hessett Bells and played darts and dominos.

I then went to work for Mr Rouse in his garage for two years, after which I came back to Hessett to work for Mr Bauly at Spring Farm. My father also worked at Spring Farm as a horseman, mainly with Suffolk Punches. Philip Friston was foreman there. Next came a job on the railway, where I stayed for a while, but couldn't settle into the work, so I came back to Mr Bauly. When I married in 1956 we moved from the Heath to a bungalow near The Green which is now part of Mount Close and when Mrs Costello's thatched cottage at the Heath burned down, she moved next door to us.

When Mr Bauly retired, I worked for Mr Mitcham. We worked from 7am with half-an-hour break for breakfast, and an hour for lunch, finishing work at 5pm. We worked longer hours in the summer than the winter due to the extra daylight. There was a harvest binder and we set the sheaves into shocks and when dry, they would be carted and put into stacks. Depending on how much there was, some might be put into the Dutch barn.

Sugar beet was pulled and the top cut off, this was hard work in the winter as it was cold and sometime frozen. Also it was piece work, so you only got paid for the work you did. We had a weekly payment equivalent to our normal wage and any extra was paid at the end of the season. The season was normally from November to February. We had a beet-lifter with two horses. We used the horses to get the beet to the sides of the field or on to a pad and Dick Renson would take them to Bury St Edmunds in his lorry. I stayed working for the Mitcham family until I retired in 1996.

I still live in the village I was born in over eighty years ago and wouldn't want to be anywhere else. I am also still enjoying the occasional visit to the Hessett Five Bells for a drink and a chat.

Graham Bauly
Malting Farm, Hessett, November 2011

I suppose my earliest memory was when I started school, I was nearly five. My first school was the East Anglian School, which was the pre-prep school for Culford which is where I went later when I was old enough. I spent three years there then I went to Culford just before I turned eight. I left Culford in 1978.

I remember my grandparents living in Malting Farm and we would go and visit them. On Sunday I went to church with nan and granddad and was confirmed at Beyton. On Good Friday granddad would sit in the middle of the room very quiet. I also went to junior church, taken by Mrs Hooper; we had a fete for the junior church which was to raise money to buy some hymn books. I used to help dad on the farm. Well, I thought I was helping, but whether or not I was I don't really know.

The men working on the farm in the late Sixties were Fred Piper, Dennis Cocksedge, who had the nickname of 'Jarpy', and Ivan Osborne. At harvest time there would be one or two retired workers helping out by stacking bales or whatever else was needed to be done. I remember a person who lived at Mount Close and his nickname was Flaker Frost. Ivy Frost who lived in number two The Green used to clean for my mother and grandmother. I went to see Jimmy Bauly and his horses as he was in the Suffolk Punch Society and was well known in the horse world.

I can remember, but not sure what age I would have been, being in the pickup truck with dad and he had to make a stop at the Hessett Bells. Dennis Medcalf, being the landlord, used to come and help out doing a bit of building work on the farm. He would also help dad with any building work on Elm Farm, where we lived at the time. I also remember the village shop but when exactly that would have been I do not know. Albert Bagg owned and ran the shop, with assistance from Sheila Hubbard and Muriel King who were working there then. Kathy Barnes opened 'Kath's Shop' a while after Bagg's shop closed and then Chris Glass took it over and renamed it 'Hessett Trading Post'.

Where Church Cottage is now, there were three thatched cottages which were in a bad way. They were renovated and made into one building and the first people to live there were a family named Hamilton, and they had four children with Neil and Robert the two younger boys. I spent a lot of holiday time playing with them on the farm. We would ride on our bikes up the road as there was not the traffic there is now; play football up against the farm walls, and on The Green. Very rarely we would go to the cinema. Once a week during the holiday time mum, my sister and I would go over and see her parents over at Creeting St Mary and spend the day with them.

Dad would go into town to the livestock market and I would go with him, which I enjoyed. Very often he would visit the Corn Exchange which I did not enjoy as I found it boring. The room was set out with tables, a merchant on each with a sample of wheat, barley or whatever we were selling. The buyer would put the corn in a slicer and take a look at the corn or just bite it and if they thought the goods were for them they would put in an offer. Now everything is analysed for just about everything! I do remember being bored by that but the livestock market was far more interesting so I only went some Wednesdays.

I also remember the St Ives Sand and Gravel lorries coming up and down the road from Hubbards Lane before I went for an interview to go to Culford. I would have been seven and dad always told the tale and up to the day before I was due to go to Culford, if anybody ever asked me what I wanted to do when I grew up it was always to be a St Ives Sand and Gravel lorry driver as there were so many lorries and they were distinctive as they had a single cab. The day I went for my interview I was not prompted in any way - I had decided I wanted to be a vet as it seemed far more appropriate than being a lorry driver, and just after that the gravel pit closed down.

After the gravel pit they set up a meat processing plant. One night there was a fire up there and the roof was asbestos which went up like fireworks and woke the whole of the village up with the fire engines going there. This made much excitement in the village. Derek Smith made lorry bodies in one of the buildings. We had him build a yellow grain trailer up there, so that would have been not long after I came back on the farm. He had been up there some years at that point so that would have been early 1980s.

I started going to Ipswich Town Football Club in about 1969/70. The first away game I went to was at Selhurst Park, Crystal Palace in London at the age of eight or nine. Ian Parris who lived in Drinkstone was friendly with dad, and it was the first game my dad had been to. I enjoyed the game more than dad did. Ian used to go regularly with Derek Prior of Woolpit. Then David Squirrell at Bradfield started taking us to games at Ipswich, I knew their oldest son Stephen fairly well. I think it was about 1971 when I had my first season ticket. David would take us to games not only at home but also a few away games, I think he was very brave taking two 10 year olds. In the mid to late 70s there was an unpleasant atmosphere at some of these games but it is definitely better now without a doubt. I appreciate David for taking us to the games and I still have a season ticket. We used to go on the old A45 which went through Beyton, Woolpit and all the villages along the way, it's easier now to get to Ipswich with the A14.

After school I worked for a year at a farm in Walsham le Willows which was called Church Farm and belonged to Martineau Farms (who still own the farm). This was a pre-college year. Martineau have had land interest in Walsham for many years, they also used to have an interest in Whitbread Breweries. I was required to do a year of practical work, and to get to work I bought an old moped scooter.

After my year was over I went to Writtle Agricultural College for a three-year sandwich course. We were two terms in college and one term out, then three terms out and one term in, with exams to be taken to qualify. It was structured so that there were two periods, both of which I worked over at Abingdon Farms, Hengrave, one time on the pig side and the other on the cattle and arable side. But the next year it reverted to one year in, one year out and one year in. I did not come back to the farm here until I had finished the course and that would have been about 1982.

I passed my driving test in April 1979 and that was half way through my work at Walsham, and I joined the Bury Young Farmers Club. Not long after that I was at college. I played football for Coldham Hall Football Club which were based at Lawshall and is still running as a club today. I also played five-a-side football, badminton and used to go to the The Bull at Thorpe Morieux once or twice a week but used to pushbike over there, where all the people I knew would meet and on a Saturday night they would have a live band. The Ship and Star in Sudbury always had a live band but I think that it has now closed. We also used to travel regularly to Ipswich to see live bands there, but that was when I had the car. I think my life started when I got a car, as I could get around and have a social life.

I had to hang up my boots when I was in my 30s as when dad became ill and I was left on the farm I became more aware that if I was to pick up an injury, I would not be able to help with the farming. I had a bit of a warning when I broke a bone in my wrist playing five–a-side football on a Friday evening and on the Monday we started the harvest and it was a bit painful and dad did not speak to me for a couple of days until he realised that I was still able to work. It brought it home to me how something like that could hinder the work, so I was lucky at not having picked up a really bad injury.

Up at Hicket Heath Farm I had pigs, albeit only on a bit of a hobby level, I suppose. But I had pedigree rare pigs, a breed called British Lop which are still around now. They were probably one of a couple of the rarest breeds and that was almost the point when I peaked at a dozen sows and I had the second largest herd of British Lops in the world. It sounds impressive to say you have the second largest herd but when it's only a dozen sows it does not sound much. There are more being bred now and it is nice to know that they are still being bred. I got to enjoy the pigs from the days of working on the farm at Hengrave and I had them when I was at college.

I bought a couple of sows at Stoneleigh and when I had several I took them to the show and sale markets, mainly to sell the extra one I had. We would take the cattle from Hengrave to the shows, they were one of the top herds of cattle in the country. They did well and that I really enjoyed. The boar would have been a local one and I also had a pedigree boar which I brought from the show and sale which gave us the pedigree stock so I did have some pedigree animals but they went in about the late 80s as they were taking up too much time.

When I first came back on to the farm, for the first couple of years we had sheep. Dad always liked sheep and they were predominantly Suffolk-cross ewes and Suffolk rams. The idea was that the sheep would be the main livestock enterprise and I would have the pigs and dad would have some pedigree longhorn cattle, so the pigs were my hobby and the cattle were dad's. The sheep were the main stock for two to three years but they were sold as dad had a bad back and with the amount of work you have to do with lambing, sheep's bad feet etc it was a great strain on your back.

We then increased the cattle numbers again. Dad was on the committee for the Longhorn Cattle Society. There was a gentleman named Joe Henson who was on there as well. His son is Adam Henson, the farmer on the BBC programme Countryfile. It came to be known that there were Longhorn cattle in Lincolnshire, left in a will to be killed. They somehow got round the will and Joe Henson bought the cattle, some went to the Cotswolds and dad had some, and some were sold on. Longhorns won the Burkes Trophy at The Royal Show, after which they were in demand. Dad died in July 1996 and I considered myself more of a stockman than an arable farmer really, I have always enjoyed the cattle more.

The Laurels was a butcher's shop, I remember the house being built. Heath Close was built by a Dutch builder and when he went out of business Mr Baker from Thurston took over. I have been on the Parish Council for about 20 years, dad was on the council and also great grandma, Sarah Bauly.

Edna Hazelwood delivered the post on her bike. One day the village was flooded, the road to Beyton and the road up to the Heath were impassable. Dad had a tractor with a bucket on the front so Edna put the post into the bucket and climbed in herself and the post was delivered. Newspaper delivery was by Joan and Phil Warman on six days a week. The Sunday newspaper was delivered by Mr Austin from Beyton and Chris Glass took over when he gave up.

Bibliography and sources

A Survey of Suffolk Parish History, Wendy Goult

Lark Rise to Candleford, Flora Thompson

West Suffolk Illustrated, H. R. Barker

Materials for a History of Hessett, William Cooke

The Manors of Suffolk, W. A. Copinger

Causes and Consequences of the First World War, Stewart Ross

The History of the Suffolk Regiment, Lieut Colonel C. C. R. Murphy

Soldiers Died in the Great War, CD Rom

The War to End Wars 1914-1918, Readers Digest

Commonwealth War Graves Commission website, www.cwgc.org

Kelly's Directory of Suffolk

White's Directory of Suffolk, William White

Parish chest of Hessett

Wills of the Archdeaconry of Sudbury

The Society for the Protection of Ancient Buildings

At the Overseer's Door, Ray Whitehand

Gazetteer and Directory of Suffolk

The Baptist Church, Rougham, J. Duncan

Suffolk Archives (formerly the Suffolk Record Office)

Suffolk Parish Pack

History of Suffolk Parishes

Census returns for Hessett

Glebe Terriers

Manorial records

Rootsweb.com for the Hoo and Bacon families